PASTIES

LINDSEY BAREHAM

PASTIES

LINDSEY BAREHAM

MABECRON BOOKS

First published 2008 by
Mabecron Books
42 Drake Circus
Plymouth
PL4 8AB

Illustrations Rebecca Cobb
Photographs Annie Hanson
Designed by Peter Bennett

Typeset in Baskerville2 BT
Printed in China
ISBN 9780953215669

10 9 8 7 6 5 4 3 2 1

Contents

CORNISH PASTIES AND ME

'For a hearty man's dinner 'tis ample fare,
With naught too little nor none to spare;
And here again it deserveth praise
That when it has vanished its virtue stays:
For it gives sweet ease to the scullery queen,
Who hath nor platters nor knives to clean.
So I wish him joy whoever he be
That first found out the Cornish Pastie.'

I met West country bookseller Ron Johns when I came to Cornwall to do a signing for my cookery book, *The Fish Store*, which revolves around a house in Mousehole, an unspoilt fishing village just three miles west of Penzance in Mount's Bay, near the tip of Cornwall in West Penwith. Ron loved the book and later, after a talk at his shop in Falmouth, when I explained the book's story and my connection with Cornwall, he asked if I would I write a book about Cornish pasties for his new publishing company. It seemed a bit cheeky for a non-Cornish person, a visitor, as they call us in Cornwall, to write a book about pasties but I decided to say yes.

I do have strong Cornish connections and have loved pasties for as long as I can remember. As a child, my father holidayed in St Agnes, on the north coast of Cornwall, and later two of his sisters and one of his brothers moved there and it became our family holiday destination. Pasties, from the village bakery in St Agnes, were part of our holiday diet and I have strong memories of queuing up to buy them hot from the oven. The smell that wafted out from that little bakery always made my mouth water (it's watering now with the memory) and it was unbearable to be sent there for bread and not have enough money to buy a pasty.

Back home in Kent, during the rest of the long school summer holidays and sometimes in the colder months, we would get up early and head off for a day at the coast. My mother's lunch picnic basket always included home made Cornish pasties, extra big ones bulging with meat and vegetables. She would wrap them in napkins to keep them hot, but the smells would gradually get stronger, wafting round the car as we drove through the countryside to Margate or Deal. We'd eat them off china plates with knives and forks (it's strictly hands-on food in Cornwall!) with pickled beetroot and salad from my dad's allotment.

Years later, when I was old enough to go on holiday to Cornwall with my sister, we'd camp in one of our aunt's fields (she was a rare-breed chicken and pig farmer) or up by the Beacon, and live on pasties. Pasties from the St Agnes Bakery were perfect for our picnic on the beach, could be heated up for supper, and we probably had pasties for breakfast. One of my Sunday jobs as a child was to make the pastry for the inevitable apple pie, so when I left home to fend for myself, I'd make pasties instead of pies because they didn't need a pie dish and there was no washing up. As fate would have it, I married someone brought up in Cornwall, so got to know all the best places to buy pasties in and around Mousehole, which was to become my new Cornish love. Later, when I had a family of my own, I too would make pasties for my sons' picnics and their school lunch box. I didn't stick to the traditional steak filling, but used whatever I had to hand and it was the surprise filling inside the crumbly, buttery pastry that made them so successful.

Over the years I've always made pasties, particularly for picnics, but when I return to Cornwall, which I do often, I rarely make them. That's because wherever you are in the south-west Peninsula, Cornish pasties are on sale every day of the year. If you are lucky, they will be home made by the owner of a seaside café or a specialist bakery such as Ann Muller's famous Lizard Pasty Shop at Helston, on the eastern land, as we call the Lizard in Mousehole. Much as I love the classic pasty filled with potatoes, onion and steak, I am increasingly inspired by Spanish empanadas, with their exotic, lively fillings.

This little book is my take on Cornish pasties and I hope you will find it inspiring. After all, you don't have to be Cornish to love pasties and you don't have to be Cornish to make them.

Lindsey
Bareham

June 2008

THE HISTORY OF THE PASTY

To paraphrase the cookbook *Cornish Recipes Ancient and Modern*, first published by the Cornwall Women's Institute in 1929, it is said that the devil would never dare to cross the River Tamar into Cornwall, for fear of ending up as a filling in a Cornish pasty. There is confusion about the origins of what we call a Cornish Pasty but they have been associated with Cornwall for a long time. The Cornwall Records Office in Truro has a recipe for a Cornish pasty of 1746 but Les Merton, author of *The Official Encyclopaedia of the Cornish Pasty*, claims the pasty was around in Cornwall as early as 8000BC, 10,000 years ago. It's worth noting, however, that pasty is an old English word for a meat pie or pye made without a dish. The use of the word died out regionally but, perhaps due to the construction of the railways in Cornwall in the mid-1800s, it survived in the South West, particularly in Cornwall, where a meat turnover became known as a Cornish pasty. The most popular explanation is that the pasty evolved to meet the needs of tin mining, a once great, but virtually extinct Cornish industry. It's a neat theory: the pasty was an inexpensive complete meal for the miners to take to work for their midday food and usually consisted of meat trimmings, potato, onion and swede (known as turnip in Cornwall) encased in the pastry. The thick seam running over the top or round the sides of the pasty was the handle for holding it while eating, to avoid being poisoned by the arsenic likely to be found on the miner's hands. It is also often claimed that some pasties had two fillings, meat and vegetables on one side and fruit on the other. I find this hard to believe for all sorts of practical reasons and the only evidence of such a pasty is the Bedfordshire Clanger (see page 41). Marking individual pasties with the owner's initials is thought to have originated at this time as a means of identifying the right pasty for the right man. It's a tradition that continues, particularly at home to meet particular requirements, and is a simple practical way of identifying commercially made pasties, adding a V for vegetarian, P for pork, and so on.

The pasty certainly became the staple diet of Cornish miners, but also of all working men – engineers, black-smiths, farmers and fishermen but it's interesting to know that Cornish fishermen – would never take a pasty on board their boats for fear it would bring bad luck. Quite why, no one seems to know. After the collapse of the Cornish tin mining industry in the 1900s, it was the miners emigrating from Cornwall that led to the pasty's national and international spread. Where the Cornish settled, they made pasties and their descendants and friends made variations on the classic filling. Pasty making spread back up country throughout the UK and all over the world, particularly to parts of Canada and America, Mexico, South Africa, Australia and Argentina, where they call them empanadas. Carol Trewin, in her book *Gourmet Cornwall* published by Alison Hodge, even discovered a small enclave of pasty aficionados in Japan, who learnt their skills from the great Japanese potter Shoji Hamada. Hamada worked for many years with Bernard Leach at his pottery in St Ives, where he also learnt to make pasties, exporting the recipe to Japan in 1924.

Today the Cornish pasty is enjoying a renaissance and Cornwall is dotted with specialist bakers producing excellent pasties, all claiming to make the best and most authentic. These days pasties are packed with a huge variety of fillings and come in various sizes. In 1985 a group of Young Farmers in Cornwall spent seven hours making the then record pasty, over 32ft long. Such is the passion that the Cornish pasty provokes; there is even a World Pasty Championship. There has been a long debate about whether a pasty can be called Cornish if it is not made in Cornwall and in 2008 it prompted Keith Makepeace of the Soar Mill Cove Hotel, near Sal-combe in Devon, to issue a challenge to the region's pasty makers. The traditional, vegetarian and junior classes were all won by Devon residents but the overall winner was Cornish. The last word went to Cornish chef Kevin Viner, ' A pasty is a simple food to make. You only need a few good ingredients to make one of the best traditional local foods.' Indeed. The pasty is now Cornwall's most successful export and for many is the great-est symbol of Cornwall.

A WORD ABOUT MY OTHER CORNISH COOKBOOK:
THE FISH STORE

 When my sons inherited their father's childhood home, a converted pilchard factory in a small Cornish fishing village, I thought it would be a good idea to record some of the recipes and memories associated with this unusual place. It started as a notebook for their eyes only but soon turned into a journal of stories and anecdotes about the comings and goings at the Fish Store and the changing life of Mousehole, an unspoilt fishing village just three miles westward from Penzance in Mount's Bay, near the tip of Cornwall in West Penwith.

Ben John, Zach and Henry's father, was four when the family arrived from France to set up home in 'Mowzal', as the village name is pronounced, and there are colourful childhood stories of growing up in a small fishing village. In those days Mousehole was a working village with cobblers, carpenters, masons, net and crab pot making, a butcher, baker and the harbour full of big fishing boats. The war years and rationing imposed limitations but Betty, my sons' paternal grandmother, taught herself to cook from the markets of Paris and knew how to make much out of little and bring variety to the abundance of fresh fish and crabs at her disposal. Then, as now, there was sorrel, wild watercress and blackberries for free and basic vegetables available from nearby inland farms.

There are photos of their great-grandfather, the notorious bohemian early twentieth-century painter Augustus John, in the harbour. Ben has vivid memories of dreading the command to sit for a painting and then escaping to the rocks for a crab picnic and swim at Dicky Daniel's Cove. Another branch of the John family also lived in Mousehole during the late forties and early fifties and returned years later when Zach and Henry were toddlers. I wanted to record the story of their great-uncle Casper, when he was an Admiral, steaming into the bay on an aircraft carrier, accompanied by a flotilla.

By the time Zach was born in 1978, the charms of the Fish Store and village life had entered my blood. Over the years I developed my own way of dealing with the generous supplies of seafood that come our way from local fishermen and began to introduce my own cooking style into the house. As our two sons grew up, we would spend at least a month in the summer at the Fish Store and often visit for Easter and Christmas, sometimes with family and friends.

These days the Fish Store is one big open plan living space with three large windows looking out to sea. We watch the fishing boats chugging past as the transforming light plays tricks with the view. On sunny days the magical light turns the sea into shimmering gold and in the winter, when the storm winds howl across the bay, the dark, angry sea is covered with white horses.

I love the place whatever the weather and whatever the time of year but when the sun streams through the open front door and there is the promise of a crab picnic and fresh fish for supper, there is nowhere I would rather be.

Christmas is a special time in Mousehole. The harbour is filled with floating lights and a Celtic cross twinkles from St Clement's Isle – a small rocky island where once an ancient hermit was said to live – which lies a few hundred yards from the shore. The night before Christmas Eve is celebrated as Tom Bawcock's Eve in the pub when a humungous Stargazy Pie, the legendary Mousehole fish pie with pilchards poking through the top, is served to patrons of the Ship Inn on the quayside. With the Fish Store windows open wide, we can hear the open-air carol service in the harbour as we sit by the fire and look out to sea with delicious cooking smells whirling round the barn-like room.

Christmas at the Fish Store wouldn't be complete without sea bass, usually caught by Jake Freethy, skipper of Go For It, a state-of-the-art fishing boat jointly owned by Ben. We like this elegant fish cooked Chinese-style with ginger and spring onions or with balsamic vinegar and a mound of home-made game chips cooked in olive oil and tossed with chives. New Year's Eve is usually quiet in Mousehole, so after a particularly luscious fish pie, made extra special with chunks of hard-boiled egg and masses of chopped parsley in a sauce enriched with clotted cream, we might head off to St Ives for the traditional fancy dress street party.

Mousehole has plenty of its own traditions. One used to be all the children walking over the fields to Lamorna on Good Friday. We prefer walking the daffodil-strewn coastal path which winds past the Mousehole Cave – the place where old smugglers hid their contraband goods which they brought over from France in their fishing boats - and ending up at the Wink pub for one of their delicious crab sandwiches.

The Fish Store started out as a tribute to the memories of a re-markable house with an interesting background but took its own momentum, telling the story of my own on-off and on-again relationship with the Fish Store and the village of Mousehole. But it is the food, the favourite ways of cooking mackerel, monkfish and sole and how to make mayonnaise to go with a sink full of crabs waiting to be boiled and picked, then turned into bisque or Betty's crab jambalaya, which is for everyone to enjoy.

The Fish Store by Lindsey Bareham, published by Michael Joseph/Penguin.

THE CLASSIC CORNISH PASTY

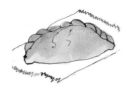

The Fish Store Cornish Pasty
The Lizard Pasty Shop Cornish Pasty
Jane Grigson's Cornish Pasty
Caroline Conran's Cornish Pasty
Marguerite Patten's Cornish Pasty
AWT'S Cornish Pasty
Mark Hix' Cornish Pasty
Dan Lepard's Steak, Swede and Mustard Pasties
Betty's Wartime Corned Beef Pasty
Marwood Yeatman's Cornish Pasty

'Pastry rolled out like a plate,
Piled with turmut, tates and mate,
Doubled up and baked like fate,
That's a Cornish pasty.'

So What's an Authentic Cornish Pasty?

The Cornish never refer to their pasties as Cornish pasties. A pasty, pronounced parsty, like lardy, with a long 'a', is just called a pasty and everyone understands that the filling will be the traditional small amount of steak, potato and onion, usually swede too. If you want a pasty with a filling other than the classic combination, and that includes minced steak, you ask for a cheese pasty, or chicken, or whatever. When times are lean and steak is replaced by potato, the Cornish pasty is historically known as a tiddy oggy, tiddy being a local name for potatoes and oggy being a west country word for pasty.

The Filling

There is also no such thing as the definitive recipe for a Cornish pasty or turnover, but everyone seems to agree that the 'classic' filling is a lowly cut of beef steak, either flank, skirt or chuck, known locally as 'pasty meat', onion, floury main crop potatoes and often swede too, known, confusingly, as turnip in Cornwall. These ingredients tend to be available all year round. The exact proportions and how they are prepared is hotly debated, even between members of the same family. Arguments rage over the 'correct' way to cut these classic ingredients. The meat is always chopped, never minced, but what size chunks make a good pasty? And what proportion of meat to vegetables and should the meat all be lean? And what about the vegetables? Should the potatoes be sliced or diced? My personal preference is for finely chopped onion, small pieces of swede and sliced potatoes, so there is less chance of them piercing the pastry. I like the meat cut quite small but I like quite a bit of it, sufficient to know that it's a steak pasty but not so much that it turns into a steak pie. Spreading the ingredients through the pasty so the meat isn't stuck at one end and the flavours are evenly distributed is achieved by piling ingredients on top of each other and seasoning between layers, rather than mixing them together beforehand. This balancing act helps ensure the pasty is juicy as well as tender. To be truly authentic, the ingredients must be Cornish. Seasoning is kept to a minimum: just salt and pepper, although some cooks add fresh or dried herbs but neither is really necessary. Aficionados would insist on black pepper for flavour and white pepper for pungency.

Cooked or Raw Ingredients?

Cooked ingredients are never included in a classic Cornish pasty. It was invented as a convenience product: convenient for the cook – everything is chopped and bundled in pastry and left in the oven to do its thing – as well as convenient to eat. Ingredients are always fresh and raw, cooking harmoniously together inside their pastry case. While the pastry cooks and hardens around the filling, an alchemy between the starch in the potatoes and swede, the moisture in the onion and the juices in the meat intermingle resulting in a surprisingly tasty moist filling with all the ingredients separate yet clinging together.

What About the Double Ended Pasty?

'There is a widespread view, particularly among our visitors, that a true Cornish pasty should have jam or apple in one end and meat and vegetables in the other. They are genuinely disappointed when their search for one is in vain. I have never met anyone who has made or eaten such a pasty, though I have seen two recipes, one in a little booklet compiled by members of St Gwinear Church, the other in British Cookery by Lizzie Boyd. There may be others, but I have found no mention of such pasties in historical records.'

Hettie Merrick, The Pasty Book,
published by Tor Mark, Redruth

I too have never seen a double-ended fruit and meat pasty but I did spend a whole day trying to make one and failed miserably. Apart from the need for savoury and sweet ingredients that cook at the same rate or to make it with pre-cooked food, it is impossibly fiddly to make a pastry bridge between the two parts that will stay in position and prevent the two fillings from leeching into each other. It is far better to follow the acknowledged tradition of using any leftover pastry to make little fruit pasties for pudding, or to make a so-called 'split' or 'windy' pasty(see page 80). This is a butter-spread fold of pastry baked unglazed which billows as it cooks, and is then split and spread with cream and jam or stewed fruit. Also see Bedfordshire Clanger, page 41.

The Pastry Case

The pastry for a pasty must be stretchy and thick enough to reach over a plump filling without tearing, although tears can be patched with leftover pastry stuck with water. The pastry must end up tender on the inside but deliciously crusty on the outside. Most people these days make (or buy) short-crust pastry, using self-raising or plain flour and lard or a mixture of lard and margarine or butter. Some people make their pastry with suet and there is a tradition of using beef dripping or lard, and flaking rather than rubbing it into the flour, so the pastry ends up puffy but not as puffy as puff pastry. This type of pastry is called rough-puff pastry and it makes the best pasty pastry of all. As to the flour, it's widely thought that plain flour, or strong plain flour (the sort used for bread making) gives the best results. Rolling the pastry quite thickly, about the thickness of a £1 coin, gives more stretch and so does resting the pastry – allowing the gluten in the flour to stretch – before rolling it into circles. Resting the pasties before they go in the oven helps avoid shrinkage that can result in splitting the pasty and unfurling the seal.

The Ridged Seal

The way the pasty is filled affects whether the distinctive rope seam or 'handle' rests down the middle of the pasty or runs round the edge. Aficionados place the filling in the middle of the pastry circle and draw the sides up to the middle to seal and then crimp. This is quite tricky to achieve and requires practice. The result though is a pleasingly plump pasty. It is far easier to place the filling on one half of the pastry and then fold the remaining half over the top before sealing and crimping. This results in a flatter pasty, the sort sold by most commercial outlets. Some cooks rest a floured rolling pin under the middle of a pastry circle then use the rolling pin to flip the rest of the pastry forward to cover the filling before sealing and crimping. The distinctive ridge or 'handle' was once a practical means for miners to hold their portable lunch and avoid being poisoned by arsenic on their fingers. These days, it's a matter of taste and appetite whether to eat the seam.

The Finish

For a glossy, appetising finish, the pasty is painted with milk, beaten egg or egg wash – a mixture of the two - before it is baked. The old Cornish habit of initialling the pasty – a means of identification for the miners – is now a way of recognising some commercially produced pasties. 'V', for example, stands for vegetarian. At home, however, it's fun to put initials on pasties.

How to Cook a Pasty

It is very important to cook a Cornish pasty properly and it takes about an hour, depending on how many are being cooked at the same time. Cooking begins in a hot oven, to cook the pastry, then the temperature is lowered to cook the filling. There are few worse things to eat than raw potatoes (swede and onion are pretty close second and third), and the lowly cut of beef steak preferred will be tough and inedible if the cooking has been hurried. The desired result is a golden crust of pastry that crumbles in the mouth and gives onto a well-filled, moist and tender filling.

How to Eat a Pasty

A pasty is a meal-on-the-hoof, the ultimate convenience meal to clutch hot between two hands. It's always sensible to go easy when you first bite into a pasty. The filling will be extremely hot if it's fresh from the oven and pasties hold their heat incredibly well, for a surprisingly long time, particularly if individually wrapped in a paper bag then rolled in a newspaper or towel for a picnic later.

I usually break the pasty in half and gauge its temperature before taking a bite but other people get stuck right in and work sideways. Cunningly, the filling stays semi-stuck together, so it won't all fall out once you start eating.

Reheating a Pasty

Place on a baking sheet and cook in a warm oven – 300F/150C/ gas mark 2 – for 10-15 minutes. Any longer and the pasty begins to dry out.

The Recipes

For a dish that involves so few ingredients and is so common all over the United Kingdom and eaten every day in Cornwall, it is amazing how many 'correct' recipes there are for a Cornish pasty. I offer my own, the recipe we follow at The Fish Store, and a selection of other favourites. The devil is in the detail.

The Fish Store Cornish Pasty
Makes 4 large, 6 'small' pasties

for the pastry:
250g/½ lb block of lard
450g/1lb strong plain flour
pinch of salt
approx 6 tbsp ice-cold water to mix

for the filling:
400g/14oz beef skirt or flank, or chuck steak
200g/8oz onion
200g/8oz swede
600g/1lb 4oz floury potatoes
1 egg whisked with 1 tbsp milk
knob of butter

Place the piece of lard in its wrapper in the freezer and leave for about an hour until very hard.

Meanwhile, prepare the filling ingredients and arrange in four equal piles, keeping each one separate. Trim and dice the beef, cutting away gristle but leaving fat, into 20p size pieces. Peel, halve and finely chop the onion. Peel and dice the swede into slightly smaller pieces. Slice the potato thinly in 5p size pieces.

Sift the flour and salt into a mixing bowl. Remove the lard from the freezer, peel back the paper, dip into the flour and grate it into the bowl, dipping back into the flour every now and again to make the grating easier. Now, mix the lard evenly into the flour by making sweeping scoops with a palette knife until it resembles heavy breadcrumbs. Stir in 1 tbsp water at a time until the dough clings together, then form it into a ball. Place the dough in a polythene bag and chill in the fridge for 30 minutes.

Divide the pastry into four equal pieces. Dust a work surface with flour and roll one pastry ball into a 20-23cm/8-9ins circle, using an upturned plate as a guide. Roll the other three pieces. Leaving a 2cm/1ins border, sprinkle onion and swede over half the pastry. Season with salt and pepper. Cover with the meat and then with half the potato. Season again and then add the remainder of the potato. Paint the border with water then fold the rest of the pastry over the filling. Press the edges together to seal (or use the tines of a fork) and then, working from one end to the other, crimp with your fingers, rolling the pastry border upwards and forming little pleats, tucking neatly as you go. Tuck the ends underneath.

Line a baking sheet with baking parchment or butter it thoroughly, and sprinkle with water. Transfer the pasties to the baking sheet with space between them. Rest for 30 minutes. Prick the top of the pasty a couple of times with a fork (to make steam holes) then brush with egg wash. If liked, use pastry trimmings to cut out the initials of the people who will be eating the pasties and 'glue' then seal with egg wash on the side of the pasty.

Heat the oven to 400F/200C/gas mark 6 and bake for 15 minutes. Lower the temperature to 300F/150C/gas mark 2 and cook for a further 45 minutes until golden and the wonderful pasty aroma is wafting round the kitchen.

Recipe from *The Fish Store* by Lindsey Bareham, published by Michael Joseph/Penguin

The Lizard Pasty Shop Cornish Pasty
Makes 4 pasties

> *'Going out for the day? Then you must take*
> *A Cornish pasty - only Ann can make.*
> *For information - you should be told,*
> *You can eat it hot - enjoy it cold.*
> *The memory of it will never fade,*
> *'Ave a Pasty proply made!*
> *Treat yourself - get on the line,*
> *Ring The Lizard (01326) 290889'*

Years ago I made a special journey to try one of Hettie Merrick's famous home-made pasties from the Lizard Pasty Shop on the Lizard Peninsula. These days Mrs Merrick's daughter, Ann Muller, runs the distinctive yellow shop and this is her highly prized recipe, as championed by Rick Stein in his *Food Heroes* series on the BBC. The pasties can be ordered by mail order and sent anywhere in the UK.

for the pastry:
100g/4oz lard
100g/4oz hard margarine (such as Stork or Echo)
450g/1lb strong plain flour (such as Doves organic)
pinch of salt
175g/6oz water

for the filling:
450g/1lb beef skirt or chuck steak
250-350g/8-10oz swede
750g/1½ lb potatoes
225g/8oz onion or shallot
1 beaten egg or milk, to glaze

For the pastry, put the lard and margarine into the freezer and leave until very hard. Meanwhile prepare the filling. Trim any gristle off the meat and cut it (with the fat) into 5mm/¼ ins pieces. Chop the swede into similar-sized pieces. Peel and slice the potatoes and chop the onion. Sift the flour and salt into a bowl and grate in the lard and margarine straight from the freezer. Gently mix through the flour and then stir in the water, 1 tbsp at a time, with a round-bladed knife until the mixture comes together. Turn it out onto a lightly floured surface and knead briefly into a ball. Wrap in clingfilm and chill for an hour.

Pre-heat the oven to 350F/180C/gas mark 4. Cut the pastry into 4 even-sized pieces, shape each one into a ball and then roll out one piece into a 20-23cm/8-9ins circle. The pastry will now be the right thickness. Place an upturned plate over the pastry and cut out a neat round. Repeat with the rest of the pastry.

Put most of the swede and onion in a line across each pastry disc and season with salt and pepper. Cover with the meat, making sure it goes right to either end, season lightly, then top with most of the potato and the rest of the swede. Season again with salt and add the rest of the potato. Very lightly brush half the circumference of the circle with water, then bring the edges together over the top of the pasty and press together. Working from right to left (or the other way if you're left-handed), fold over the corner and then fold over the edge, towards yourself, working from one end of the pasty to the other, creating a rope-like design to seal. Tuck in the other end well. Chill for 1 hour.

Make a small slit in the top of each pasty, then brush with beaten egg or milk and place on a greased and floured baking sheet, leaving 5cm/2ins between each one. Bake for 1 hour.

Recipe from *Rick Stein's Food Heroes*, BBC Books.

Jane Grigson's Cornish Pasty

Makes 2 or 4 pasties

One of my favourite cookery writers who specialised in British regional cooking.

for the pastry:
400g/12oz plain flour
175g/6oz lard
ice cold water

for the filling:
500g/1lb rump or chuck steak, or skirt
125g-150g/4-5oz onion, chopped
90g/3oz turnip or swede, chopped
250g/8oz potato, peeled and thinly sliced
good pinch of thyme
beaten egg to glaze

Make a firm pastry in the usual way and roll out two dinner plate circles or four side plate circles according to whether you are feeding two ravenous people or four of moderate appetite. Leave to chill while you prepare the filling. Cut all the skin and gristle from the meat, and chop it. There should be at least 300g/10oz of skirt, rather more of better quality steak.

Season and layer the filling ingredients to one side of the pastry circles. Or mix them together (traditions differ). Brush edges with egg, flip over the pastry to form a half-moon shape, and twist the edges to give a rope effect. Mark initials, if you have varied the filling, in one corner. Brush over with egg and make two small holes at the top for the steam to escape. Bake at 400F/200C/gas mark 6 for 20 minutes, then lower the heat to 350F/180C/gas mark 4 for a further 40 minutes. Protect the pastry with butter papers if they brown too fast.

Recipe from *The Observer Guide to British Cookery* by Jane Grigson, published by Michael Joseph.

Caroline Conran's Cornish Pasty
Makes 6 smallish pasties

300g/10oz steak, well trimmed and cut up very small
1 small potato, peeled and cut up small
1 onion, peeled and chopped finely
parsley, chopped finely
3 tbsp gravy, stock or water
350g/¾ lb shortcrust pastry made from 250g/8oz plain flour, 100g/3½oz
fat, pinch salt and water to bind
1 egg, beaten, or milk, to glaze pastry

Heat the oven to 425F/220C/gas mark 7. Mix the steak, potato, onion, parsley, salt and pepper, and moisten with the liquid. Roll out the pastry and cut out six circles with the help of a saucer.

Put a dollop of the mixture on the centre of each, brush round the edges with beaten egg or milk, and fold the pastry up, pinching the edges together in a pretty serpentine pattern.

Place on a greased tin, brush with more beaten egg or milk, prick the tops with a fork to let out the steam and bake in the top of the oven for 10-15 minutes to cook the pastry; then turn the oven down to 300F/150C/gas mark 2, and, depending on the quality and tenderness of the steak, bake for a further ½–1hour. To reheat, put for 15 minutes in a low oven.

Recipe from *Poor Cook* by Susan Campbell and Caroline Conran with illustrations by Susan Campbell, published by Macmillan.

Marguerite Patten's Cornish Pasty

Makes 4 pasties

Marguerite Patten OBE was one of our first celebrity cooks, teaching the nation how to survive on war rations.

for the pastry:
350g/12oz plain white flour
175g/4oz fat, all butter, all margarine or half butter or margarine and half lard
4-6 tbsp ice cold water

for the filling:
350g/12oz rump steak
2 medium potatoes
2 medium onions
¼ medium swede, optional
few mixed chopped herbs, optional
2-3 tsp beef stock
1 beaten egg

Sift the flour and salt into a mixing bowl. Cut the fat/s into pieces and drop into the flour. Lift some of the fat and flour with your fingertips, or forefingers and thumbs, and rub together. Continue until the mixture looks like fine breadcrumbs. Gradually add the liquid and blend with the dough, using a flat-bladed knife, continuing until the mixture is easily formed into a ball and leaves the bowl clean. Rest for 30 minutes before rolling.

Heat the oven to 425F/220C/gas mark 7. Grease a large baking tray. Roll the pastry and cut into 4 rounds about the size of a tea plate or large saucer. Cut the meat into 1.5cm/½ins squares. Peel the vegetables and cut into slightly smaller dice. Blend the meat with the vegetables, seasoning and herbs, if using. Moisten with the stock. Place the filling in the centre of the pastry rounds. Moisten the edges with water and bring them together to form the upright pasty shape. Seal firmly and flute the edges. Lift carefully on to the baking tray. Brush with egg wash. Bake for 15 minutes then lower the heat to 325F/160C/gas mark 3. Bake for a further 30 minutes.

Recipe from *Classic British Dishes* by Marguerite Patten, published by Grub Street.

AWT'S Cornish Pasty
Makes 2 very large pasties or 4 modest ones
The Cornish got very upset when Antony Worrall Thompson cooked his version of a Cornish pasty on television. This is a modified version, modified by him, 'to appease them'. I wonder how many people know that Tony is in fact Cornish.

450g/1lb shortcrust pastry (ideally made with lard)
450g/1lb chuck steak
140g/5oz onion, finely diced
100g/4oz swede, peeled and thinly sliced
175g/6oz potato, peeled and thinly sliced
½ tsp fresh soft thyme leaves
pinch cayenne pepper
½ tsp ground black pepper
¼ tsp salt
1 beaten egg

Preheat the oven to 200°C/400°F/gas mark 6. Roll out the pastry and cut out two circles the size of dinner plates, about 23 cm (9 in) in diameter. Trim the meat of any sinew, gristle or fat. Cut the meat into 5 mm (¼ in) dice and combine with the onion, swede, potato, thyme, peppers and salt. Arrange the meat mixture down the middle of each circle of pastry, leaving 2.5 cm (1 in) at each end. Brush the edges of the circles with a little of the beaten egg.

Either bring the two edges together over the meat or fold one side over to meet the other. Pinch or crimp the pastry together to make a tight seal and place on a baking sheet. Brush with the beaten egg. Cook the pasties for 20–25 minutes, then reduce the heat to 160°C/325°F/gas mark 3 and cook for a further 40 minutes. Serve hot or cold.

Mark Hix' Cornish Pasty
Makes 6-8 pasties
For years Mark Hix was the executive chef of Caprice Holdings, owner of the fashionable Ivy restaurant, but he's a west country lad who grew up in Dorset. He reckons pasties are making a comeback. Not that they've ever gone away, he says, but now there are some seriously good pasty companies making Cornwall's answer to fast food. Being a chef – or is it because he comes from Dorset? – Mark cooks his pasty ingredients first and the result is a deluxe gourmet pasty. His latest restaurant is Hix Oyster and Chop House in Smithfield, London's meat market.

for the filling:
200g/8oz swede, peeled and cut into rough 1.5cm/¾ins pieces
1 large baking potato, peeled and cut into rough 1.5cm/¾ins pieces
2 tbsp vegetable oil
2 onions, finely chopped
500g rump or rib steak, trimmed of fat and chopped into 5mm pieces
250ml/9fl oz beef stock (cube is fine)
1 tbsp Worcestershire sauce

for the pastry:
500g/1lb flour
2 tsp salt
125g/4½ oz butter, chilled and cut in small pieces
125g lard, chilled and cut in small pieces
a little milk to mix
1 egg, beaten, to seal and glaze

To make the filling, heat half the oil in a large heavy frying pan and gently cook the onions for 2-3 minutes until soft. Remove from the pan and put to one side. Heat the pan again over a high heat, add the rest of the oil, season and add the meat. Cook over a high heat for 3-4 minutes, turning, until evenly browned. Add the meat to the onions. Add the stock to the pan with the Worcestershire sauce, and boil rapidly until 2-3 tbsp of liquid is left. Return the meat and onion and simmer until the sauce is reduced and coats the meat. Meanwhile, cook the potatoes and swede in separate pans of boiling water until just tender, then drain and mix into the meat.

To make the pastry, mix flour and salt together then rub the butter and lard into the flour with your fingers, or mix in a food processor, until it has the texture of fine breadcrumbs. Mix in some milk, 1 tbsp at a time, until a smooth rollable dough forms that leaves the sides of the bowl clean. Roll the pastry on a lightly floured board to a thickness of about 3mm and, using a plate or bowl as template, cut out 6 circles about 18cm/7ins in diameter. Spoon the filling evenly in the centre of the 6 discs of pastry. Brush round the edges with beaten egg and bring the edges of the pastry up around the filling, then crimp the edges together with

your fingers, or roll the edges back over and then crimp down.
Brush the tops with the remaining egg mixture and cut a small
slit in the top for steam to escape. Chill for about 30 minutes.

Heat the oven to 400F/200C/gas mark 6. Bake the pasties for
20 minutes then turn the oven down to 360F/180C/gas mark 4
and cook for a further 20 minutes or until golden. If browning too
fast, cover with foil.

Recipe from *British Regional Food* by Mark Hix, published by
Quadrille.

Dan Lepard's Steak, Swede and Mustard Pasties
Makes 5 pasties
Dan Lepard is a baker extraordinaire.

for the pastry:
300g/12oz plain flour plus extra for rolling
75g/3oz strong white flour
50g/2oz unsalted butter, softened
150g/6oz beef dripping, at room temperature
about 125ml/5fl oz ice-cold water
2 egg yolks

for the filling:
250g/10oz frying steak, preferably rump
175g/7oz peeled swede and potato (half each)
freshly mixed Colman's mustard

Place the two flours and ½ tsp salt in a mixing bowl. Cut the butter in small pieces and rub through the flour. Cut the dripping
into 1cm/½ins cubes and toss these through the flour. Beat the
water with the yolks to combine, then stir this through the flour
with a fork until it forms a dough in the bowl, adding a little more

water if needed. Leave for 30 minutes. Flour the work surface and roll the dough to measure about 50cm x 20cm (20ins x 8ins). Fold the dough in by thirds then roll out again and fold in the opposite direction. Cover the dough, leave in a cool place for 30 minutes, then repeat the two sets of rolling and folding.

To make the filling, lightly freeze the steak and cut into 1cm/½ins cubes. Chop the swede and potato into small pieces. Toss these ingredients with 1 tsp salt, ¾ tsp white pepper and 1 tbsp plain flour. Roll the pastry to about 5mm thick and cut into rounds using a small side plate. Spread the middle of the pastry lightly with mustard, brush a 5mm border with water and place a generous spoonful of filling on one side of the pastry disc. Fold the pastry over the filling and press to seal. Place on a baking tray and chill while you heat the oven to 400F/200C/gas mark 6. Bake for 45 minutes until golden.

From *British Baking* by Dan Lepard, www.danlepard.com, published by Fourth Estate.

Marwood Yeatman's Cornish Pasty
Makes 4 pasties

for the pastry:
450g/1lb plain flour
110g/4oz lard
110g/4oz suet
pinch of salt

for the filling:
450g/1lb skirt of beef
1 large potato
200g/8oz swede
1 onion
dripping

Make the pastry by rubbing the lard into the flour and salt, adding the suet and mixing to a dough by gradually adding 150ml/5floz of ice cold water. Rest in the larder. Peel potato, swede and keep in water. Chop up the meat and onion finely. Divide pastry into 4 and roll into 23cm/9ins circles. Pare equal amounts of potato into the middle of each pastry circle then swede. Put the onion and meat on top. Dot with dripping and season well.

Now comes the tricky bit. Brush the rim with water and gather it up into a sausage. Holding the pasty in shape with one hand, press the edges together with the forefinger and thumb on the other. This, with practice, will get you an upper crust. By shifting the ingredients, you can achieve one on the side. Heat the oven to 400F/200C/gas mark 6 for 40 minutes. Eat wrapped in a napkin the customary way – standing up.

From *The Last Food of England, English Food: Its Past, Present and Future* published by Ebury Press.

Betty's Wartime Corned Beef Pasty

Makes 1 pasty

During the war, when beef was hard to come by, pasties were made with canned corned beef. The result is quite different from a regular pasty because the chunks of meat melt as it cooks, imbuing the potatoes with a rich, luscious, meaty sauce.

for the pastry:
50g/2oz margarine or lard
100g/4oz self-raising flour
cold water

for the filling:
1 small onion
1 medium potato
150g/6oz corned beef

Rub the fat into the flour then stir with 1-3 tbsp cold water to bind. Rest while you peel and dice the onion and potatoes. Cut the corned beef into small pieces. Mix everything together and sprinkle with a little salt. Roll out the pastry, using a plate as a template. Put the filling in the middle. Moisten the edges with water, then bring the pastry over the filling, pressing to seal. Crimp then bake at 350F/180C/gas mark 4 for 45 minutes.

HITHER AND YON

Wakes Pasties
Forfar Bridies
Priddy Oggy
Bedfordshire Clanger
Kentish Pork, Sage and Apple
Chicken, Bacon and Mushroom
Pork Empanadas from Tucuman
Beef Empanadas
Brazilian Prawn Empadinhas

'The exodus of Cornish mining skills from the 1840s onwards led to the world-wide spread of pasties as a food item. For the descendants of those original emigrants to Australia, South Africa, Canada and America, the Cornish pasty is deeply embedded in their memories, and they jealously guard its recipe and traditions.'

This chapter of the book captures other pasties from around the British Isles, including some of my own, and variations from hither and yon, most particularly the empanadas from Spain and South America, which are the closest equivalent of the Cornish pasty.

There are traditions of wrapping small bundles of food in pastry all over the world but all are much smaller than the Cornish pasty. Many, including Russian pirozhki and Polish kapusniaczki are made with yeast pastry, and often served with soup. In Greece, Turkey and Croatia, little pastry turnovers, called borek, are made with flaky filo pastry, piled, layer on layer, to build up a pale, triangular soft case for all manner of fillings. These fillings are always delicate and well minced, and might be local cheese,

spinach or leeks and sometimes aubergine, sweetbreads or meat. In India, a similar triangular pastry is called a samosa, but it's deep-fried rather than baked. In the Lebanon, sambousak are pasty shaped but small, about 10cm/4ins long, with a deep frill. Traditional fillings such as minced lamb fried with chopped onion and pine nuts, flavoured with cinnamon, or spinach with onion and pine nuts, flavoured with resinous sumac and lemon, and grated halloumi with flat-leaf parsley and melted butter are per-fect for pasty fillings . The pastry for these 'pasties' is made with flour and vegetable oil, flavoured with salt and sugar and, like borek, they are deep fried. In Apulia in Italy, where the cuisine is dominated by olive oil, they make a delicious turnover with pizza dough and stuff it with Parma ham, mozzarella and Parmesan. They call it panzerotti and fry it in olive oil.

Wakes Pasties
Makes 2 pasties
I once wrote an article for SAGA magazine about grandparents cooking with their grandchildren. In the course of my research, I came across *Grandparents' Cook Book*, recipes collected by students of *City of London School for Girls*. That's where I found this recipe from Laura Hibbert of Bolton, Lancashire.

'From its origin as an all-night vigil before holy days the wake became, espe-cially in northern England, linked to celebrations and travelling fairs. In Westhoughton, near Bolton, Lancashire, 'Wakes Week' was not the annual holiday connected with the cotton mills but the week including August 24, the feast of St Bartholomew, the patron saint of the Parish Church, for which Wakes Pasties were traditionally baked. My late sister, Alice, born in 1911, a baker and confectioner by trade, used to include a small china figure of a female child, no doubt in origin a fertility symbol, as these were often also baked into Christening cakes.'

for the pastry:
225g/8oz plain flour
pinch of salt
75g/3oz butter
25g/1oz lard
4-6 tbsp cold water

for the filling:
450g/1lb lean minced beef
1 onion, chopped
25g/1oz dripping or vegetable fat
1 tbsp flour
½ pint stock
beaten egg, for glazing

Fry beef and onion in a large pan. Sprinkle flour over and stir in stock. Simmer for 40 minutes – 1 hour. Cool. Halve the pastry, roll into two circles on a floured surface, crimp as described in the Classic Cornish Pasty, (page 14). Brush pasties with beaten egg. Cook for about 25 minutes (190C) or until golden.

Grandparents' Cook Book by students of the City of London School for Girls, copies £15.00 from Don Kehoe, 1 Sebastian House, 2-4 Sebastian Street, EC1V 0HE. Cheques made out to: City of London for Girls Bursary Fund.

Forfar Bridies

Makes 4 pasties

A bridie is the Scottish version of a pasty but made in a horseshoe shape, the whole shoe, rather like a deep pasty. The edges are finished differently too: first given a 'dunt' by pressing down with the heel or the hand and then a 'nick' or crimp using the forefinger and thumb. This is Sue Lawrence's recipe, from her book *Scots Cooking*, published by Headline.

for the pastry:
250g/9oz strong white flour
75g/3oz plain flour
75g/3oz unsalted butter, diced
75g/3oz white fat

for the filling:
450g/1lb shoulder or rump of beef
75g/3oz beef suet, grated
1 small onion, peeled and finely grated

Sift the flours and a pinch of salt into a food processor. Add the fats and process until incorporated. Add just enough cold water (about 3 tbsp) to bind to a stiff dough. Gather up with your hands, wrap in clingfilm and chill for an hour.

Roughly chop the meat or use the pulse button on your food processor to mince it roughly. Mix together the beef, suet, onion and plenty of salt and pepper. The mixture should be fairly stiff. Divide the pastry into 4 and roll each piece into an oval. Spoon the filling onto one half of each pastry oval, leaving a border. Dampen the edges of the pastry, fold the uncovered half over the filling to enclose it. Trim the edges into a neat horseshoe shape. 'Dunt' the edges by pressing with the heel of your hand and 'nick' by crimping with forefinger and thumb. Use a knife to prise a small hole for the steam to escape. Place on a buttered baking tray, chill for an hour and bake for 35-40 minutes or until golden brown in a hot oven, 400F/200C/gas mark 6.

Priddy Oggy
Makes 8 pasties
In 1968, Paul Leyton, the landlord of the Miners' Arms in Priddy,
Somerset, invented a pasty for his pub and called it the Priddy
Oggy, using the Cornish word for a pasty. The pastry is made with
cheese and the filling is pork, bacon, more cheese and a dash of
Tabasco, although these days there are many claims on the original recipe. This is *the* original, given to Jane Grigson by Mr Leyton, published in *The Observer Guide to British Cookery* (which also
has a stunning photo of Stargazy Pie which originated in Mousehole). Eccentric, perhaps, but delicious, yet easy to simplify.

for the pastry:
30g/1oz each butter and lard
100g/3½ oz mature Cheddar, grated
2½ tbsp water
pinch salt
250g/8oz flour, sieved

for the filling:
1 pork tenderloin, weighing about 600g/1¼ lb
about 35g/generous 1oz smoked pork, bacon or Bayonne ham,
sliced very thinly
90g/3oz mature Cheddar, grated
sprig of parsley, chopped
8 drops of Tabasco
1 large egg, beaten

To make the pastry, put the fats into a warmed bowl and cream
them. Add Cheddar, water and salt, mixing well. Cool until firm,
then rub into the flour roughly. Take about 125g/4oz of this crumbly mixture and roll it into a slab 1cm (½ ins) thick. Repeat and,
after moistening the top with a brush dipped in water, place each

slab on the previous one. Press the pile firmly, then cut downwards into 125g/4oz slices, around 4 slices – and repeat the process twice more. Chill for 30 minutes. Cut into 8 pieces, squeeze each into a sausage and roll out into a circle measuring 15cm/6ins in diameter. Chill again for an hour.

Trim the tenderloin of its bits and pieces of skin. Divide it into two lengthways, making two long pieces, and beat each piece gently until it is about ½cm/¼ins thick. Divide the smoked pork slices into eight strips. Make the cheese stuffing by mixing cheese, parsley, salt and Tabasco and adding half the egg yolk. Spread this over the surface of the tenderloin. Roll each piece up and chill until firm, preferably in the deep freeze. They should not be frozen hard, just very firm.

Put the oggies together, cut each roll of tenderloin into four, and wrap a strip of smoked pork around each one. Lay the little parcels in the middle of the pastry circles. Brush the edges with milk or water. Bring the pastry edges up and over the pork, pressing them together in a scalloped crest. Trim and press the whole thing down to make a flat base. Brush over the remaining egg yolk (add 1 tsp water if a bit on the short side). Bake for 10 minutes in the oven preheated to 350F/280C/gas mark 4, until the pastry begins to brown. Deep fry until they are brown, or fry in a merest bit of lard, turning to brown evenly.

Before cooking, they can rest in fridge for 3 days, or in a deep-freeze for 3 months. In the latter case, let them thaw before cooking.

Bedfordshire Clanger
Makes 2 clangers
A Bedfordshire Clanger is probably the apocryphal double-ended
pasty that everyone always associates with Cornish miners. It
started out as a boiled suet roll, with meat as the filling and fruit
dotted through the suet roll, but evolved into a suet crust pastry
with savoury and sweet ingredients at opposite ends. This recipe,
using regular shortcrust pastry, comes from Bedfordshire County
Council's website. Good luck!

450g/1lb shortcrust pastry (see page 91)
1 beaten egg
2 tsp granulated sugar

for the savoury filling:
1 small onion, chopped
1 tbsp lard
225g/½ lb minced pork
1 tsp dried sage
1 cooking apple
50g/2oz cooked peas

for the sweet filling:
2 dessert apples
50g/2oz dates, stoned and chopped
grated rind of 1 orange
55g/2oz (generous) sultanas
2 tbsp caster sugar

Preheat the oven to 425F/220C/gas mark 7. To make the savoury
filling, fry the onion in the lard in a frying pan for a couple of
minutes until soft and golden. Stir in the pork and sage and cook
gently, stirring often, for 5 minutes. Peel, core and chop the apple

gently, stirring often, for 5 minutes. Peel, core and chop the apple and add to the pork mixture. Cook for a further 5 minutes, then stir in the peas, season to taste and leave to cool.

To make the sweet filling, peel and chop the apples, then place in a mixing bowl and stir in the chopped dates, orange rind, sultanas and sugar.

Roll out the pastry to about 5mm thick and cut out two circles, 25cm/10cm in diameter. Re-roll the trimmings, and cut out two thick 12.½cm/5ins x 1cm/½ ins strips. Brush the long edges of each strip with a little beaten egg and stand one strip on its long side from the edge of the centre of each circle, to form a wall. Make the strip stand up by pressing the bottom edge quite firmly onto the circle. Brush the edges of the circles all the way round with beaten egg. On one side of each pastry wall, put half of the savoury filling, and on the other side put half of the sweet filling.

Fold the other half of each pastry circle over the filling to form a pastry shape, and press the centre lightly so that the dividing strip sticks to the top. Pinch the edges firmly together, brush each clanger with the rest of the beaten egg and sprinkle with sugar. Bake the clangers for 15 minutes, then lower the heat to 375F/190C/gas mark 5 and bake for a further 25 minutes. Serve hot.

Kentish Pork, Sage and Apple
Makes 4 medium, 6 small pasties
A very simple pork pasty adapted from a pie my mother used to make.

1 quantity pastry (see page 88) or 500g/1lb puff pastry
flour for dusting
400g/12oz lean pork
1 onion, approx 200g/8oz
1 cooking apple, approx 400g/12oz

2 tbsp lemon juice
4 fresh sage leaves or 1 tsp dried sage
1 egg beaten with 1 tbsp milk, for glazing

Dice the pork quite small. Peel and grate or finely chop the onion. Peel, quarter and finely slice across the quarters directly into a mixing bowl with the lemon juice, tossing as you go. Finely chop the sage. Mix all the ingredients and fill, crimp and glaze, then bake in the usual way (see page 52).

Chicken, Bacon and Mushroom
Makes 4 pasties
Don't be put off by the addition of mayonnaise; it combines with smooth Dijon mustard to hold the ingredients in a luscious creamy sauce. Good hot or cold.

1 quantity of pastry (see page 88) or 500g/1lb puff pastry
4 rashers smoked streaky bacon
½ tbsp cooking oil
125g/5oz spring onions
250g/½ lb chicken fillet, preferably thigh
200g/8oz chestnut mushrooms
1 tsp smooth Dijon mustard
1 tbsp mayonnaise
1 beaten egg, for glazing

Chop the bacon and cook to a crisp in the oil. Meanwhile, trim and finely slice the spring onions, including all the green. Dice the chicken. Wipe and slice the mushrooms. Stir the spring onions into the bacon, reduce the heat and cook gently for 2-3 minutes until limp. Increase the heat slightly and add the chicken, tossing around until evenly coloured. Stir in the mushrooms and toss until damp-looking and beginning to wilt and darken. Cool to tepid. Mix the mustard into the mayonnaise and stir through the mixture. Roll the pastry, cut out four circles and proceed as described on page 52.

Empanadas

Empanadas are the Spanish equivalent of pasties but these turnovers are smaller and eaten as a snack rather than a meal. They were discovered centuries ago in Galicia but countless Galician emigrants have taken their speciality to every part of Spain and throughout South America. The pastry is softer and the cooking faster than Cornish pasties, and the fillings tend to follow the seasons, whilst reflecting regional specialities. In north west Argentina, for example, potatoes are added; in some places, peas.

In La Rioja they add olives; in Tucuman, the empanadas are smaller and made with chicken or pork and many vegetables; in Patagonia, lamb, shrimp or hare meat is common, and in Cordoba the empanadas are sweeter and larger. I offer three recipes. The first is a spicy pork and egg filling, sweetened by raisins and sharpened with chilli from the Tucuman, adapted from *Argentine Cookery* by Maizal Ediciones.

The closest equivalent to the traditional Cornish pasty, or turnover, is the ubiquitous Argentinian beef empanada, made with chilli and green olives. My version is made with prime rump steak chopped into tiny pieces. The flavouring is superb, and a delicious combination of beef, pimiento-stuffed green olives, red onion and green pepper, with a hint of garlic and chilli. Because it is a cooked stuffing, any pastry is suitable but I would recommend my version of empanada pastry or the delectably crumbly egg shortcrust pastry. The third filling is my favourite, made with prawns, and inspired by one I found in *Street Café, Brazil*, by (sadly missed) Michael Bateman. Also see Family Pasties page 62, for three Galician recipes for empanada pies; the fillings could also be used to make individual turnovers.

Pork Empanadas from Tucuman
Makes enough for a party

for the pastry:
1kg/2lb 4oz flour
250g/10oz melted fat
1tsp salt dissolved in 1 cup cold water

for the filling:
1kg/1lb 2oz pork loin cut into very tiny cubes
600g/1lb 4oz chopped onions
300g/12oz chopped spring onions
250g/10oz fat
60g/2oz raisins
3 hard-boiled eggs, chopped
1 tbsp chopped red pepper
1 tsp finely chopped chilli

To make the pastry, pour the melted fat into the dough and mix
all the ingredients to make a stiff dough. Leave, covered, to prove
for 1 hour, then roll 12cm/4½ ins discs, approx 3mm thick. Rest
before filling.

Put the meat in a sieve and pour boiling water through it, fol-
lowed by cold water. Leave to drain. Soften the onions in the fat
and then add the meat. When cooked, season with salt and pepper.

Chill then stir in the remaining ingredients. Fill, seal, crimp
and bake in a very hot oven for 10-12 minutes (see page 21 for
more details)

Beef Empanadas
Makes 6 small empanadas

½ quantity empanada pastry (see page 90)
for the filling:
1 green pepper, approx 125g/5oz
1 red onion, approx 150g/6oz
2 garlic cloves
generous pinch chilli flakes
1 tbsp olive oil
15 pimiento-stuffed green olives
250g/6oz rump steak
2 tbsp red wine or water
beaten egg to glaze

Trim, de-seed and finely chop the pepper. Peel, halve and finely chop the red onion and garlic. Heat the olive oil in a frying pan and gently soften the onion, pepper and garlic with the chilli flakes, stirring occasionally and allowing about 20 minutes in total. Meanwhile, halve the olives lengthways and slice across the halves to make 3 pieces per half. Trim the steak and cut into dolly mixture size pieces. When the onion mixture is soft, increase the heat slightly and stir in the meat. Toss until all the pieces have browned. Add the olives and wine or water. Allow the juices to simmer into the meat, cooking for 5-10 minutes until moist rather than wet. Tip into a bowl to cool. Roll the pastry into 6 pieces, approx 15cm/6ins. Working on one empanada at a time, paint a 1cm/½ins border with water and place a spoonful of filling on one half of the pastry. Fold over the empty pastry, press the edges to seal then crimp and proceed in the usual way (see page 21). Bake at 360F/180C/gas mark 4 for 25-30 minutes until golden.

Brazilian Prawn Empadinhas
Makes 12-20 empadinhas

1 quantity empanada pastry (see page 90)
175g/6oz peeled prawns
1 crushed garlic clove
juice of 1 lime
olive oil for frying
350g/12oz finely chopped onions
1 finely chopped green pepper
250g/9oz skinned and seeded tomatoes or
400g/14oz can chopped tomatoes, drained
1 tsp tomato puree
1 tbsp chopped coriander
12 chopped black olives
1 tsp cornflour
1 beaten egg

Chop the prawns and mix with the garlic and lime juice. Leave
for 30 minutes. Soften the onions and pepper in 2 tbsp olive oil.
Add tomatoes, puree and coriander and cook for a couple more
minutes before adding the prawns and juices, 2tbsp water and the
black olives. Simmer for a few minutes while you slake the cornflour with 1 tbsp water. Stir this into the mixture until thickened.
Leave to cool. Roll out the pastry on a floured board to about
3mm/⅛ ins thickness, proceed as previous recipe with extra help
on page 21.

CHEATS' PASTIES

Potato and Cream
Spicy Chickpea and Potato
Ploughman's Pasty
Cheese and Apple with Membrillo
Goat's Cheese and Leek
Spring Greens with Mascarpone
Prawn and Pea with Feta
Rick Stein's Crab with Leek and Saffron
Smoked Haddock, Leek and Clotted Cream
Russian Salmon and Dill
Mushy Peas and Smoked Bacon
Sausage and Apple
Steak and Mushroom

'It was said that the devil would never dare to cross the River Tamar into Cornwall for fear of ending up as a filling in a Cornish pasty'.
Cornish folklore

When I was doing research for this book, talking to families in Mousehole and upcountry in St Agnes, which are 'my' two parts of Cornwall, several Cornish ladies told me they often cheat and use ready-made pastry for their pasties. That was music to my ears, because I do it all the time. After all, we love things wrapped in pastry in my house, and calling leftovers a pasty (or empanada) is smart housekeeping. I particularly like puff pastry for these impromptu pasties because it cooks quickly and gives spectacular results.

If cooking a cheat's pasty from scratch, choose fillets of tender meat, not stewing cuts, and slice them small or thin. Raw food

must be seasoned with salt. This encourages the food to be juicy
as well as sharpening up the flavours. Onions, which are essen-
tial for moisture, must be grated or sliced wafer-thin, or choose
spring onions. I often use canned Eazy fried onions, which are
chopped and cooked to the molten stage in olive oil, for quick
pasties. Many supermarkets sell them or ring 01372 375444 for
your nearest stockist. Potatoes and other root vegetables must be
sliced on a mandoline or cut crisp-thickness. Mushrooms work
well but must be thinly sliced. If you think the filling will end up
dry, add a scoop of thick cream. Be aware too that raw fillings
usually shrink with cooking so it is important to be extra generous and tuck snugly when using puff pastry because the pastry
lives up to its name and has a tendency to billow away from the
filling. Seafood, particularly hot smoked and leftover cooked
salmon, or crab, mussels, sardines and smoked mackerel, with
something creamy to hold everything together, is well suited to a
crisp, flaky pastry covering. Some fillings, like Rick Stein's luscious crab pasty with leek and saffron, are a mixture of cooked
and raw ingredients.

You can buy puff and short crust pastry in various forms, from
thick slabs to ready rolled circles and oblongs. It's available
frozen, chilled or preserved in some way that it doesn't require re-
frigeration. Roll it in the usual way, on a floured work surface and
aim for pastry that is the thickness of a 50p coin, slightly thinner
than normal. I find it easier to make smaller pasties with soft but
stretchy puff pastry and use a 15cm/6ins or 18cm/7ins saucer as a
guideline. 500g/1lb puff pastry will make 6 small pasties
and 4 large ones. Be generous with the filling, piling it on half the circle of pastry, the closest to
you, but leave more border than you think

necessary – at least 2.5cm/1 ins. Paint the border with water to glue the pastry after you piled on the filling, fold over the pastry flap, gently juggling to fit, then press to seal with your fingers, paint the seal sparingly with water and then, working from left to right (if you are right-handed), or right to left (if you are left-handed), quickly and neatly turn the edge in small tucks to make the distinctive ridged finish. Get creative with your crimping and develop your own style, just ensure that the scalloped edges go upwards, to avoid the juice from escaping.

I think puff pasties look particularly appetising with a glossy finish but that's an optional extra. You could use milk or a mixture of beaten egg and milk or just beaten egg. Don't forget to prick the pasties a few times with a fork to make air holes and thus avoid them building up a head of steam that is likely to result in burst pasties. Transfer the pasties to a baking sheet lined with non-stick baking parchment or grease it thoroughly before transferring the pasties. Bake in a hot oven – 400F/200C/gas mark 6 – for 20-30 minutes until puffed and golden. Big appetites will probably need two - of both sizes.

Unless stated otherwise, follow these directions for making the following recipes.

Potato and Cream
Makes 2 medium pasties
Bite into creamy slices of potato heaven, a sort of pommes
Dauphinoise in pastry. This is also good with a little chopped
thyme or rosemary, a hint of garlic and/or scraps of ham or bacon.

200g/8oz puff pastry
flour for dusting
2 shallots or small onions
2 potatoes, approx 200g/8oz in total
4 tbsp thick cream
beaten egg, for glazing

Have the pastry discs rolled. Peel, halve and slice the onion wafer-
thin. Peel the potato and slice very thinly, as if making thick
crisps. Leaving a 2.5cm/1in border, fill one side of the pastry by
making a layer of onion, then potato. Season with salt and pepper,
add a dollop of cream and repeat the layers. Brush the border
with water and quickly fold over the flap of pastry, gently juggling
to fit. Press all round the edge with your fingers to seal, paint the
seal sparingly with water and then, working from left to right (if
you are right-handed), or right to left (if you are left-handed),
quickly and neatly turn the edge in small tucks to make the distinctive ridged finish. Paint with egg wash and prick a few times
with a fork. Transfer to a baking sheet lined with baking parchment, and bake in a hot oven (400F/200C/gas mark 6) for 20-30
minutes until the pastry is puffed and golden.

Spicy Chickpea and Potato
Makes 6 pasties
Curried carbohydrates.

500g/1lb boiled new potatoes
200g/8oz canned Eazy fried onions or 200g/8oz softened chopped onion
1 roasted red pepper (from a jar)
400g/14oz can chickpeas
3 tbsp vegetable oil
sugar lump of fresh ginger
1 garlic clove
½ tsp chilli flakes
1 tsp each turmeric, cumin and coriander

3 tbsp mango chutney
1 tbsp lime or lemon juice
2 tbsp chopped coriander
500g/1lb puff pastry
flour for dusting
1 beaten egg, for glazing

Chop the potatoes into sugar-lump size dice. Chop the pepper. Tip the chickpeas into a colander and rinse with cold water. Fry the onion and pepper together in a large frying pan for about 5 minutes. Meanwhile, keeping separate piles, peel and finely chop the garlic and ginger. Sprinkle the garlic with a little salt and use the flat of a knife to work to a paste. Stir both into the onions with the chilli flakes and cook for a couple of minutes before adding the turmeric, cumin, coriander and ½ teaspoon of salt. Cook, stirring constantly, for about 30 seconds. Add the chickpeas, potatoes, mango chutney and 4 tablespoons of cold water.

Stir thoroughly and simmer for a couple of minutes for the flavours to mix and mingle. Add the coriander and lime or lemon juice. Stir again and leave to cool before using. Proceed as for previous recipe, page 52.

Ploughman's Pasty
Makes 4 medium, 6 small pasties
Potatoes, onion, cheese and chutney has never tasted so good.

500g/16oz puff pastry
flour for dusting
300g/12oz cold boiled potatoes
200g/8oz mature Cheddar
150g/6oz canned Eazy fried onion or 150g/6oz softened chopped onion
3 tbsp Branston or other pickle or chutney
1 beaten egg, for glazing

Peel and chunk the potatoes. Grate the cheese. Mix all the ingredients together. Proceed as for potato and cream, page 52.

Cheese and Apple with Membrillo
Makes 4 medium, 6 small pasties

Membrillo is golden brown quince paste stocked by most supermarkets. It's very sweet and has a subtle but powerful concentrated apple-meets-pears flavour, with a pleasing grainy texture. It melts but doesn't disintegrate with heating. In Spain membrillo is served with cheese and any cheese is suitable for this recipe.

500g/1lb puff pastry
flour for dusting
500g/1lb Bramley cooking apples
1 small lemon
200g/8oz strong Cheddar, Comte, or other farmhouse cheese
100g/4oz quince paste/membrillo
1 beaten egg, for glazing

Squeeze the lemon juice into a mixing bowl. Peel, core and quarter the apples. Slice across the quarters thinly, stirring them into the lemon juice as you go. Dice the cheese and toss with the apple. Pile the filling onto the pastry as usual, layer and top with thin slivers of membrillo. Proceed as for potato and cream, page 52.

Goat's Cheese and Leek
Makes 4 medium, 8 small pasties

500g/1lb puff pastry
flour for dusting
300g/12oz trimmed leek
1 garlic clove
25g/1oz butter
1 tbsp vegetable oil
2 tbsp chopped flat leaf parsley
200g/8oz Camembert goat's cheese
1 beaten egg, for glazing

Have the pastry discs ready. Slice the leeks thinly in rounds. Rinse and shake dry. Peel and finely chop the garlic. Melt the butter with the oil then stir in the leek and garlic. Season with salt and pepper, cover and cook for 4 minutes. Stir in the parsley and set aside to cool. Cut the cheese in chunks without removing the rind. Divide the leeks between one half of the pastry circles leaving a 2.5cm/1ins border. Cut the cheese in chunks and arrange on top. Continue as usual, see page 52.

Spring Greens with Mascarpone
Makes 4 medium, 6 small pasties
Pretty, elegant and very tasty.

500g/1lb puff pastry
flour for dusting
7 spring onions
knob of butter
100g/4oz young spinach
160g/6oz frozen petits pois and soya bean mix, or all frozen petits pois
100g/4oz boiled salad potatoes
2 tbsp mascarpone or thick cream
100g/4oz Greek feta
1 beaten egg, for glazing

Trim and finely slice the spring onions, including all the green.
Soften in the butter. Tip into a mixing bowl. Meanwhile, using
water from the kettle, crush the spinach into boiling water and
boil for 1 minute. Scoop into a colander to drain. Drop the frozen
veg into the boiling water and boil for 2 minutes until tender.
Drain. Squeeze all the water out of the spinach. Slice through the
ball of spinach to chop. Chunk the potatoes. Mix the spinach,
peas, potatoes and mascarpone into the onion. Crumble the feta
over the top and mix again. Proceed as for potato and cream,
page 52.

Prawn and Pea with Feta
Makes 4 medium, 8 small pasties

500g/1lb puff pastry
flour for dusting
125g/5oz spring onions
knob of butter
200g/8oz frozen peas
2 tbsp thick cream
100g/8oz peeled prawns
100g/8oz Greek feta cheese
1 beaten egg, for glazing

Trim and finely slice the spring onions, including all the green.
Soften in butter. Use water from the kettle to boil the peas for a
couple of minutes until tender. Drain. Puree in a food processor
with the cream. Scrape into a bowl and mix with the spring
onions and prawns. Crumble the feta over the top. Mix again.
Chill. Proceed as for potato and cream, page 52.

Rick Stein's Crab with Leek and Saffron
Makes 6 pasties

900g/2lb chilled fresh puff pastry
½ tsp saffron strands
2 tsp hot water
225g/8oz leeks
350g/12oz white crab meat
75g/3oz brown crab meat
50g/2oz fresh white breadcrumbs
1 tsp salt
10 turns of the white pepper mill
25g/1oz butter, melted

Heat the oven to 200C/400F/gas mark 6. Divide the pastry into 6 pieces. Roll out each piece on a lightly floured surface and cut into a 19cm/7½in circle.

For the filling, soak the saffron in the hot water for 5 minutes. Thinly slice the leeks, rinse and shake dry. Put the white and brown crab meat, leeks, breadcrumbs, salt and pepper into a bowl and stir together until well mixed. Crush the saffron a little into the water to release the colour and flavour, then stir it into the melted butter. Now stir this into the rest of the filling ingredients.

Divide the filling mixture between the pastry circles. Brush the edge of one half with a little water, bring both sides together over the top of the filling and pinch together well to seal. Crimp the edge of each pasty decoratively between your fingers, transfer to a lightly greased baking sheet and bake for 35 minutes, until golden brown. Serve hot or cold.

Recipe from *Fruits of the Sea* by Rick Stein, BBC Books. Crab pasties are sold at Stein's Patisserie, 1 Lanadwell St, Padstow, tel 01841 532700

Smoked Haddock, Leek and Clotted Cream
Makes 4 medium, 6 small pasties

500g/1lb puff pastry
400g/16oz naturally smoked haddock fillet
200g/8oz leek white
400g/16oz boiled potato
4 tbsp clotted cream
1 beaten egg, for glazing

Cook the fish in sufficient water to cover, simmering for a few minutes until just tender. Drain and flake the fish into a mixing bowl. Finely slice the leek and add to the bowl together with the diced potato and cream. Season with black pepper and stir. Chill. Proceed as for potato and cream, page 52.

Russian Salmon and Dill
Makes 4 medium, 6 small pasties
A lovely combination of creamy, dill-flecked rice and chunks of
salmon. Good cold.

500g/1lb puff pastry
flour for dusting
75g/3oz long-grain rice
7 spring onions
knob of butter
120g/5oz salmon flakes (roast, poached or hot smoked)
1 tbsp chopped dill
3 tbsp thick cream
1 beaten egg, for glazing

Boil the rice in plenty of water for 10 minutes or until tender. Tip
into a sieve to drain. Meanwhile, trim and finely slice the spring
onions, including all the green. Soften in butter. Tip the drained
rice into a mixing bowl. Add the spring onions, flaked fish, dill
and cream. Mix. Proceed as for potato and cream, page 52.

Mushy Peas and Smoked Bacon
Makes 4 medium, 6 small pasties

500g/1lb puff pastry
flour for dusting
100g/4oz smoked streaky bacon
1 tsp vegetable oil
300g/10oz can minted mushy peas
100g/4oz canned Eazy fried onion or 150g/6oz softened chopped onion
100g/4oz boiled waxy potatoes
1 beaten egg, for glazing

Chop the bacon and fry until crisp in the vegetable oil. Drain excess oil. Mix the bacon into the lightly crushed peas with the onion and chunked potatoes.

Sausage and Apple
Makes 4 medium, 6 small pasties
Little chunks of sausage in a creamy mustard apple sauce.

flour for dusting
4 meaty pork sausages
200g/8oz canned Eazy fried onions or 250g/10oz softened chopped onion
6 tbsp olive oil
1 Bramley cooking apple, approx 500g
1 tbsp lemon juice
1 tbsp smooth Dijon mustard
500g/1lb puff pastry
1 beaten egg, for glazing

Peel, halve and finely chop the onion. Choose a large frying/sauté pan and gently soften and lightly brown the onion in 2 tbsp olive oil, allowing about 8 minutes. Run a sharp knife down the sausages and peel away the skin. Form 8 balls from each sausage, quickly rolling between your palms. Drop the balls into the onion, increase the heat slightly and brown all over. Meanwhile, peel, core and chunk the apple. Toss with the lemon juice and add both to the browned meatballs. Season with salt and pepper, reduce the heat again, cover the dish and cook for 15 minutes, stirring half way through to encourage the apple to mush and the sausage balls to cook evenly. Stir the mustard into the apple to make a creamy sauce. Allow to cool. Proceed as for potato and cream, page 52.

Steak and Mushroom
Makes 2 medium pasties
A posh quickie, almost a classic pasty.

200g/8oz puff pastry
150g/6oz fillet or other top steak
150g/6oz potato
2 shallots or small onions
1 small mushroom
smooth Dijon mustard
1 beaten egg, for glazing

Have the pastry discs ready. Slice the steak into slivers, peel and thinly slice the potato but do not rinse. Peel, halve and finely slice the onions. Wipe the mushroom and slice wafer-thin. Start with onion, then meat, potato and mushroom, making two layers of both ingredients, seasoning lightly with salt and pepper as you go. Smear the other half of the pastry with mustard. Proceed as for potato and cream, page 52.

FAMILY PASTIES AND PASTY PIES

**Leek Pasty Pie with Clotted Cream
Cockle Empanada Pie
Beetroot, Lemon and Tomato Pasty Pie with Feta
Prawn and Spinach Pasty Pie with Goat's Cheese
Sardine Empanada Pie
Medieval Salmon
Gammon and Spinach Pasty Pie with Gruyere
Leek, Chicken and Parsley Pasty Pie
Pork and Ham Empanada Pie
Lamb and Apricot Moroccan Pasty Pie
Venison and Mushroom Pasty Pie
Rhubarb and Clotted Cream Pasty Pie with Saffron**

*'When he needed comforting and a friendly lap, he would go to see his special
friend Bessie, who worked for his mother, and she would get a large pasty out
of the meat-safe and cut him off a slice. On a really good day, she might bring
out an apple pastry, flavoured with cloves. He would watch her cut off the
end, and pour in brown sugar and clotted cream before handing it to him.'*
Jane Grigson, English Food

I didn't realize until I started doing research for this book that
the huge Desperate Dan-size pasties that my mother used to
make for the family were common in homes all over Cornwall and
it was the 'foreigners' (like us, actually) who made individual
pasties, the sort sold in the UK today. We often had one of these
big pasties for supper, two of them divided up amongst the six of
us. There was usually an argument about who got the pointed
ends because my mum made the best short-crust pastry I've ever
eaten. The soft, crumbly texture was down to a mixture of

(mainly) lard and a little bit of margarine or butter. Her secret, she claimed, was very cold hands.

It would be easy to scale up any of the classic pasty recipes (see pages 20-32) to make large pasties or pasty pies to share but the recipes given here have fillings that are cooked in advance and chilled first. When I am feeling extra lazy, I make pasty pies. Placing one circle of pastry over another to sandwich the filling is what I mean by a pasty pie. The edge is crimped in the pasty style and divided four ways after baking, to make a pasty shape for holding in both hands or for eating on a plate with a knife and fork. This is a common practice in Galicia, where empanadas originated.

Any pastry is suitable for recipes in this section but some are particularly suited to ready-made puff pastry. For pastry recipes, see page 88.

Leek Pasty Pie with Clotted Cream
Makes 1 pasty pie, serves 4

1kg/1³⁄₄lb trimmed leeks
75g/3oz butter plus a little extra
3 tbsp clotted cream
2 x 275g/11oz round or oblong ready-rolled puff pastry
flour for dusting
1 egg beaten with 1 tbsp milk

Slice the leeks in 2cm/½ ins thick rounds. Soak in cold water for a few minutes then drain. Melt the butter in a wide frying pan, add the leeks, cover the pan and cook gently, stirring once during cooking, for about 20 minutes until the leeks are very soft. Stir in the cream, increase the heat and cook uncovered for a few more minutes until the leeks are creamy rather than wet. Spread the leeks out on a plate to cool.

Heat the oven to 400F/200C/gas mark 6. Place a baking sheet in the oven to get very hot – this ensures the pastry base cooks thoroughly. Butter a second baking sheet or spread with non-stick baking parchment. Dust a work surface and lightly roll the pastry to make 2 circles approximately 30cm/12 ins. Lay a pastry disc on the buttered baking sheet. Paint a 2.5cm/1ins border with water or egg wash and spoon the cooled leeks inside the border. Butter a baking sheet and lay out one pastry circle. Paint a 2.5cm/1ins border. Spoon the filling on the pastry going up to the border. Position the pastry lid, pressing the edges with a fork to seal. Roll the forked edge towards the middle, making small tucks as you work round the edge, crimping in the pasty style. Make a small hole in the centre, paint with egg wash then use a small knife to etch a pattern – swirling triangles radiating from the hole. Bake for 30 minutes or until the pastry is puffed, golden and spectacular.

To make the double pasties, lay out one pastry circle, paint a 2.5cm/1ins with egg wash and spoon the cooled filling on one half of the circle, going up to the border. Fold the empty half over the filling, press the edges and proceed as for the pie.

Cockle Empanada Pie

1 quantity of empanada pastry (see page 90) or
2 x 275g/11oz circles puff pastry
1kg/1¾ lbs cleaned clams or mussels
2 bay leaves
3 tbsp olive oil
2 finely chopped medium onions
2 finely chopped garlic cloves
2 finely chopped green peppers
pinch of hot paprika

Boil the clams or mussels with the bay leaves in sufficient water to just cover, until all the shells have opened, shaking the pan several times. Discard any clams that fail to open. Drain, cool and pick clams or mussels from their shells. Meanwhile, soften the onion, garlic and peppers in the olive oil. Stir in the clams or mussels. Cool before proceeding as for preceding recipe.

Beetroot and Lemon Tomato Pasty Pie with Feta

Makes 1 pasty pie or 2 double pasties

Beetroot stewed with tomatoes and lemon juices with a hint of chilli is a lovely mix of sweet and sour with a snap of chilli heat. Feta cheese adds a delicious creaminess.

450g/10oz boiled beetroot
1 small lemon
450g/10oz ripe tomatoes
2 tbsp vegetable oil
1 red onion
½ tsp cumin seeds
¼ tsp dried red chilli flakes
200g/8oz Greek feta
2 x 275g/11oz round or oblong ready-rolled puff pastry
beaten egg, for glazing

Rub the skin off the beetroot and chop into sugar-lump-size dice. Remove the lemon zest in paper-thin scraps. Peel, halve and finely slice the onion. Peel and chop the tomatoes. Heat the oil in a medium-sized saucepan over a low heat. Stir cumin seeds and chilli flakes into the hot oil, then add the onion. Cook, stirring frequently, for about 10 minutes, until the onion is soft and slippery. Add the lemon zest, tomatoes and juice from the lemon. Season with salt and pepper and cook uncovered for 15 minutes or until the tomatoes are sloppy and the lemon zest soft. Add the beetroot and simmer for a further 15 minutes. Taste and adjust the seasoning. Chill.

Heat the oven to 425F/220C/gas mark 7. Place a baking sheet in the oven to get very hot – this ensures the pastry base cooks thoroughly. Butter a second baking sheet. Dust a work surface and lightly roll the pastry to make 2 circles approximately 30cm/12ins. For the pie, lay a pastry disc on the buttered baking sheet. Paint a 2.5cm/1ins border with egg wash and spoon the cooled mixture inside the border. Crumble the feta over the top and proceed as before(see pages 64, 65). To make two pasties, lay out the two pastry circles, paint a 2.5cm/1ins with egg wash and spoon the cooled filling on one half of the circle, going up to the border. Crumble the feta over the top. Fold the empty half over the filling, press the edges and proceed as for the pie.

Prawn and Spinach Pasty Pie with Goat's Cheese
Makes 1 pasty pie, serves 4

500g/1lb young spinach
200g/8oz peeled prawns
100g/4oz clotted cream
100g/4oz crumbly goat's cheese
500g/1lb puff pastry
flour for dusting
beaten egg, for glazing
Heat the oven to 425F/220C/gas mark 7.

Squash the spinach into a pan of boiling, salted water and cook for 2 minutes. Drain in a colander and leave to cool. Meanwhile, place a baking sheet in the oven to get very hot – this ensures the pastry base cooks thoroughly. Butter a second baking sheet or line with non-stick baking parchment. Dust a work surface and lightly roll the pastry to make 2 circles approximately 30cm/12 ins.When the spinach is cool enough to handle, squeeze tightly between your hands. Chop a few times and then slacken with the cream and mix in the prawns. Crumble the cheese over the top and mix again.

Lay a pastry disc on the buttered baking sheet. Paint a 2.5cm/1ins border with egg wash or water and spoon the filling inside the border. Season with salt and pepper. Form a lid with the second piece of pastry. Press the edges together with your fingers and then seal the border with a fork. Paint all over with beaten egg then crimp in the pasty style, making small tucks as you work round the edge. Make a few fork holes in middle of the pastry to allow steam to escape. Etch portion control marks with the point of a knife. Slide the baking sheet with the pie onto the hot baking sheet in the oven and bake for 20-25 minutes until puffed and golden.

Sardine Empanada Pie
Makes 1 pasty pie or 2 double pasties

1 quantity of empanada pastry (see page 90) or
2 x 275g/11oz circles puff pastry
6 finely chopped large onions
5 tbsp olive oil
2 finely chopped green peppers
4 beef tomatoes, skinned and diced
500g/1lb small sardines, gutted and cleaned

Soften the garlic in the olive oil. Add the peppers and diced tomato and cook until thick and sauce-like. Cool. Arrange the sardines on the prepared pastry and top with a generous covering of sauce. Proceed as for previous recipe.

Medieval Salmon

Makes 1 pasty pie or 4 medium pasties

This surprisingly delicious combination of flavours is based on a seminal medieval pie recipe combining fresh salmon with crystallised ginger, raisins and almonds. It was a star amongst a galaxy of outstanding dishes at The Hole In The Wall, George Perry Smith's restaurant in Bath which in the fifties and sixties was the best place to eat outside London. The recipe survives in numerous cook books and my version owes a debt to the revised edition of *English Food* by Jane Grigson. The original is served with a creamy mustard and shallot sauce. I give the recipe for that too but the pasties are moist and delicious enough without.

400g/12oz can pink or red wild salmon
2 pieces stem ginger
15g/½oz blanched almonds
15g/½oz raisins
75g/3oz butter
flour for dusting
250g/10oz puff pastry for the pie or
400g/12oz puff pastry for the pasties
1 egg

optional sauce:
1 large shallot or small onion
150ml/6oz white wine or white wine vinegar
1 tsp smooth Dijon mustard
2 tbsp creme fraiche
1 tbsp finely snipped chives

Break apart the big piece of fish and remove the central bone, any skin and grey fat. Break the fish into kebab-size chunks. Chop the ginger and the almonds. Mix together 50g/2oz of the butter with the ginger, almonds and raisins. Dust a work surface with flour.

Roll the pastry into two pieces 24cm/9ins x approximately 18cm/7ins, or, if making pasties, cut out 4 circles approx 15cm/6ins. Lightly oil a baking sheet and lay out one piece of pastry. Scatter fish and chunks of the butter mixture over the pastry leaving a 2.5cm/1ins border. Beat the egg and use to paint the border. Position the lid, pressing the edges together, rolling them towards the pie and then crimp with a fork to seal and secure. Make a few steam holes with the fork then paint the entire surface with egg.

Heat the oven to 400F/200C/gas mark 6. Bake in the oven for 20-30 minutes until puffed and golden. For the sauce, peel, halve and finely chop the shallot. Melt 25g/1oz butter in a small pan, stir in the shallot and cook for about 5 minutes until soft. Stir in the mustard and then add the white wine or wine vinegar. Boil, uncovered, until reduced by half. Stir in the creme fraiche and chives. Heat, stirring, to amalgamate. Crack the pasty pie and pour on the sauce or serve separately.

Gammon and Spinach Pasty Pie with Gruyere
Makes 1 pasty pie or 2 double pasties

500g/1lb young spinach
1 onion
350ml/12 fl oz milk
500g/1lb puff pastry
150g/5oz grated Gruyere Cheese
250g/10oz thickly sliced gammon or ham
25g/1oz butter plus an extra knob
25g/1oz flour
½ tbsp smooth Dijon mustard
100g/4oz clotted cream
beaten egg, for glazing

Heat the oven to 400F/200C/gas mark 6. Boil the spinach for 1 minute.
Drain and leave to cool. Roll the pastry into two circles, approx 30cm/12ins. Tear the ham into 50p size pieces. Melt the butter in a medium pan, stir in the flour, then the mustard. Add the milk, stirring to make a smooth sauce as it comes to the boil. Simmer for 5 minutes. Add the cheese and cream then leave to cool. Squeeze the spinach dry. Stir spinach and torn ham into the white sauce. Cool. Proceed as for previous recipe, page 70.

Leek, Chicken and Parsley Pasty Pie

Makes 1 pasty pie or 1 double pasty
Crisp, golden pastry gives on to chunks of chicken and soft leek held in a creamy, parsley sauce. Good cold and perfect for a picnic.

225g/8oz plain flour plus 2 tbsp extra
125g/5oz butter
3-4 tbsp cold water
2 leeks
1 shallot or
1 small onion and 1 garlic clove
400g/14oz diced chicken
150ml/6fl oz milk
4 tbsp coarsely chopped flat leaf Parsley
1 egg whisked with 1 tbsp milk

Pre-heat the oven to 400F/200C/gas mark 6. Sift 225g flour into a mixing bowl. Cut 100g butter into pieces and use your fingertips to work it quickly into the flour until it resembles heavy bread-crumbs. Stir in sufficient cold water to enable the dough to cling together. Knead lightly to form a ball. Cover and chill.
Trim and slice the leeks in 1cm rounds. Rinse and shake dry.

Peel, halve and finely chop the shallot or onion and garlic. Melt 25g butter in a spacious frying pan and stir in leeks and shallot or onion and garlic. Season with salt, cover the pan and cook for 10 minutes until the leeks are soft. Meanwhile, cut the chicken into chunks. Increase the heat and stir the chicken into the pan, stirring for a few minutes until all the pieces are white. Sift 1 tablespoon of flour over the top, stir vigorously until it disappears, then stir in the milk to make a thick, smooth sauce. Reduce the heat and cook gently for a few minutes to cook the flour. Add the parsley and check the seasoning. Cool. Proceed as before, page 70.

Pork and Ham Empanada Pie
Makes 1 pasty pie or 2 double pasties

1 quantity of empanada pastry (see page 92) or
2 x 275g/11oz circles puff pastry
4 tbsp olive oil
500g/1lb pork loin, cut into thin strips
2 finely chopped large onions
2 finely chopped garlic cloves
2 finely chopped green peppers
125g/5oz diced air-dried ham (Serrano or Parma)
2 tbsp tomato paste
1 tsp sweet paprika

Heat the olive oil in a large frying pan and quickly fry the pork. Transfer to a plate. Soften the onions and garlic. Mix in the peppers and diced ham, fry briefly then return the pork, adding the tomato paste, paprika and a decent seasoning of salt and pepper. Cool before proceeding as before, page 70.

Lamb and Apricot Moroccan Pasty Pie
Makes 2 pasty pies or 4 double pasties
There's a definite whiff of the casbah about this subtly seasoned
Moroccan filling. The luscious lamb filling is piled over cous cous.
Perfect for a pasty party.

for the filling:
2 onions
5 tbsp olive oil
50g/2oz blanched almonds
900g/1¾ lb boned shoulder lamb
3 tbsp ras al hanout (www.seasonedpioneers.co.uk)
1 tbsp ground cumin
600ml/1pt chicken stock (cube is fine)
very generous pinch saffron stamens
200g/8oz soft-dried, ready-to-eat apricots
80g/3oz bunch coriander

for the cous cous:
250ml/½pt boiling chicken stock (cube is fine)
pinch of saffron stamens
1 tbsp olive oil
1 tbsp lemon juice
150g/6oz cous cous
2 x 275g/11oz round or oblong ready-rolled puff pastry
beaten egg, for glazing

Peel, halve and finely slice the onions. Heat 3 tbsp olive oil in a
spacious, heavy-bottomed, lidded casserole dish over medium
heat. Stir in the onions, cook for a few minutes then add the almonds. Meanwhile, cut the lamb into big kebab-size pieces and
brown in a frying pan in batches in the remaining oil. When the

onions are wilted and lightly browned, add the meat and stir in the ras al hanout and cumin before adding the stock, saffron and apricots. Stir thoroughly and bring the stew to the boil. Meanwhile, chop the coriander, stalks and all. Reduce the heat to low, stir in the coriander, cover and simmer for 1 hour or until the meat is very tender. Taste and adjust the seasoning with salt and pepper. Cool then tip into a sieve to catch the gravy.

To make the cous cous, stir the stock, saffron, olive oil and lemon juice together in a bowl then stir in the cous cous. Cover and leave for 10 minutes or until hydrated. Fork up the cous cous. Cool.

To complete: heat the oven to 425F/220C/gas mark 7. Place a baking sheet in the oven to get very hot – this ensures the pastry base cooks thoroughly. Oil a second baking sheet. Dust a work surface and lightly roll the pastry to make 2 circles approximately 30cm/12ins. For the pie, lay a pastry disc on the buttered baking sheet. Paint a 2.5cm/1ins border with egg wash and spoon cous cous topped with the cooled lamb mixture inside the border. Season with salt and pepper. Form a lid with the second piece of pastry. Press the edges together. Paint all over with beaten egg and then seal the edges with a fork. Roll the edge forward towards the middle and crimp in the pasty style. Make a few fork holes in middle of the pastry to allow steam to escape. Etch portion control marks with the point of a knife.

Slide the baking sheet with the pie onto the hot baking sheet in the oven and bake for 20-25 minutes until puffed and golden. To make two pasties, lay out the two pastry circles, paint a 2.5cm/1ins with egg wash. Spoon the cous cous and then the cooled lamb on one half of the circle, going up to the border. Fold the empty half over the filling, press the edges and proceed as for the pie.

Venison and Mushroom Pasty Pie
Makes 1 large pasty pie or 2 double pasties

for the filling:
2 onions, approx 300g/½ lb in total
2 tbsp groundnut oil
knob of butter
1 bay leaf
500g/1lb venison cut into small dice
flour for dusting
300g/½ lb baby button mushrooms
few sprigs of thyme
600ml/1pt hot chicken stock
150ml/¼ pt red wine
1 dsp redcurrant jelly
2 tbsp chopped parsley

for the pastry:
400g/14oz plain flour plus extra for dusting
100g/4oz lard
100g/4oz butter
5-6 tbsp cold water
beaten egg, for glazing

Peel, halve and chop the onion. Heat oil and butter in a spacious Le Creuset-style, lidded pan and gently soften the onion with the bay leaf. Pat the venison dry and dust with flour. Scoop the onions into a sieve over the pan, so the oil drains back. Increase the heat and brown the venison in batches. Return meat and onions, add 150ml/6fl oz wine and the thyme. Stir to loosen the flour as it bubbles then add the stock, 1 dsp redcurrant jelly and wiped mushrooms. Bring to the boil, stirring, reduce the heat to very low, cover and simmer very gently for about an hour or until the meat is tender. Season with salt. Leave to cool then remove bayleaf and thyme stalks. Drain most of the gravy into a jug.

Heat the oven to 425F/220C/gas mark 7. Oil a baking sheet. Dust a work surface and lightly roll the pastry to make 2 circles approximately 30cm/12ins. For the pie, lay a pastry disc on the oiled baking sheet. Paint a 2.5cm/1ins border with egg wash and spoon the cooled mixture inside the border, moistening with some of the gravy. Continue as preceding recipe, page 73.

Rhubarb and Clotted Cream Pasty Pie with Saffron
Makes 1 small pasty pie

Cornwall used to be famous for saffron and this explains the other speciality of the Cornish bakery: the saffron cake. This yellow currant loaf or bun is delicious toasted and spread with clotted cream and jam. In this pasty filling, rhubarb is cooked in orange juice and honey with a hint of saffron. Delicious hot or cold, it is best eaten from a plate because it's a bit juicy!

600g/1lb rhubarb
200ml/8fl oz fresh orange juice
pinch saffron stamens softened in 1 tbsp boiling water
2 tbsp runny honey
500g/1lb puff pastry
flour for dusting
knob of butter or ½ tbsp vegetable oil
150g/6oz clotted cream
beaten egg, for glazing
1 tbsp caster sugar

Pre-heat the oven to 425F/220C/gas mark 7. Trim and chop the rhubarb. Simmer very gently, covered, in a sauté pan to retain the shape of the chunks, with orange juice, saffron and honey until soft. Leave to cool then drain the juice into a jug. Roll the pastry and cut two circles approximately 20cm/8ins. Butter a baking sheet. Cover with one circle and egg paint a 1cm/½ins border. Thickly spread the cream over the pastry, going up to the border. Add the rhubarb and cover with the second circle of pastry. Crimp the edges with a fork. Paint with egg. Roll the edge forward and crimp in the pasty style. Pierce at the centre then etch a few radials. Sprinkle with sugar. Bake for about 20 minutes until puffed, crisp and golden.

PUDDING PASTIES

Splits
Date
Mincemeat with Fresh Cranberries
Dutch Apple
Blackberry and Apple
Frozen Raspberries and Custard
Plum with Crystallized Ginger
Plum with Almond Cream
Apricot and Goat's Cheese with Cardamom

'The Cornish pasty contributes £150 million a year to the Cornish economy.'

Pudding pasties are usually called turnovers. At home, they are generally smaller than savoury pasties because they tend to be made with leftover pastry trimmings. Anything goes, from apple with butter and a dusting of sugar, pear with blue cheese or a handful of strawberries with clotted cream. The danger, of course, with juicy soft fruit, is that their juices will dribble through the crimping and air holes as they cook. In Cornwall there is a tradition of making 'splits' from leftover pasty pastry and treating them like scones, splitting the puffed 'windy' pastry in half and spreading it with butter, clotted cream or jam, or all three. I like making very small fruit pasties – more like little empanadas – to serve hot from the oven for pudding with clotted cream or Cornish ice cream.
Also see Family Pasties, page62.

Splits

Makes about 10

I found this recipe for Cornish splits in *Country Recipes of Old England* published in 1929, a delightfully illustrated book belonging to one of my Cornish aunts. Underneath, there's a quaint line drawing of a skinny tuxedoed man doing the splits.

500g/1 lb flour
pinch salt
15g/½ oz yeast
1 tsp caster sugar
25g/1oz butter
300ml/½ pt milk

Add the salt to the flour, mix the yeast with the sugar, dissolve the butter in the milk and, when tepid, pour it over the yeast, then mix the flour to a dough. Leave in a warm place until well risen, knead again and shape into rounds approx 1cm/½ ins thick.

Brush with milk and bake at 350F/180C/gas mark 4 for about 15 minutes until risen. Cut through, spread with butter or clotted cream, and jam.

Date

Makes 10 small, two-bite pasties

If you are lucky enough to live near a middle-eastern shop where they sell big, soft, sweet medjool dates, they would be perfect for these simple yet simply delicious flattened pasties. But remember them too, when you are wondering what to do with last year's Christmas dates. The buttery, softened hot dates are particularly good in rough puff pastry but shortcrust is better than puff. Eat with clotted cream.

300g rough puff or shortcrust pastry
10 medjool or 20 regular dates
25g/1oz butter
egg wash (egg beaten with a splash of milk)

Roll out the pastry and cut out 10 circles approx 7cm/3ins diameter. Split the dates and remove the stone, leaving a 1cm/½ins border, snuggle the date halves on half the pastry, dot with butter, paint the border with a little water, fold over the other half, pressing lightly all over, then crimp the edges. If liked, and it's fiddly, attempt a pasty finish by turning the edge in small tucks to make the distinctive ridged finish. Paint with egg wash and prick a few times with a fork. Transfer to a baking sheet lined with baking parchment, and bake in a hot oven (400F/200C/gas mark 6) for 20-30 minutes until the pastry is puffed and golden.

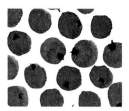

Mincemeat with Fresh Cranberries
Makes 20 small, two-bite pasties
These are a lovely idea at Christmas: little empanada-style simply crimped pasties piled on a plate, dusted with icing sugar and decorated with a sprig of holly.

500g/1lb shortcrust pastry
200g/8oz mincemeat
3 tbsp fresh cranberries
egg wash

Roll out the pastry and cut out 20 circles approx 7cm/3ins diameter. Mix the mincemeat and cranberries. Leaving a 1cm/½ins border, spoon mincemeat on one half of the circle. Working on one pasty at a time, paint the border with a little water and proceed as for date pasties.

Dutch Apple (or Apple and Goji Berry)
Makes 6 medium pasties
Any apple is suitable for these pasties but eating apples will retain
their shape whilst Bramleys or other cooking apples will soften in
a fluffy way. I prefer the latter and like to dot the apple with butter, sugar and a squeeze of lemon to make the flavours more interesting. Dutch apple, for some reason, refers to sultanas.

Pretty pink goji berries, which are rather like elongated sultanas, are a great alternative. They are the most nutritionally
rich food on the planet, containing 500 times more vitamin C
than oranges and the highest content of carotenoids, including
beta carotene, of all foods on earth.

500g/1lb pastry
2 Bramley apples
1 tbsp lemon juice
3 tbsp sultanas or goji berries
40g/scant 2oz butter
2 tbsp demerara sugar
egg wash

Roll the pastry and cut 6 circles approx 15cm/6ins. Peel, core and
chunk, slice or grate the apple. Toss with lemon juice and mix
with the sultanas. Leaving a 2.5cm/1ins border, pile the apple on
one side of the circle. Top with slices of butter and a sprinkling of
sugar. Proceed as for date pasties, page 81.

Blackberry and Apple
Use preceding recipe, replacing sultanas with a handful of ripe
blackberries.

Frozen Raspberries and Custard
Makes 6 medium pasties

500g/1lb puff pastry
200g/8oz chilled thick custard
200g/8oz frozen raspberries
2 tbsp clotted cream

Roll out the pastry to make 6 circles, approx 15cm/6ins. Working quickly, on one pasty at a time, leave a border approx 2.5cm/1ins and spoon a dollop of custard on one half of the circle. Top with raspberries and a scoop of cream. Proceed as for date pasties, page 81.

Plum with Crystallized Ginger
Makes 6 small pasties

300g/12oz puff pastry
9 plums
2 pieces of stem ginger
2 tbsp juice from crystallized ginger
25g/1oz butter
sugar

Roll out the pastry and cut out 6 circles approx 10cm/4ins diameter. Cut the plum off the stones in big chunks and then into small pieces. Chop the ginger and mix plums and ginger. Working on one pasty at a time and leaving a 2.5cm/1ins border, pile plums and ginger on half the circle. Cut scraps of butter over the top and dredge with sugar and moisten with crystallized ginger juice before proceeding as for date pasties, page 81.

Plum with Almond Cream

Makes 6 pasties

Juicy, soft plums against a buttery, sugary almond cream and no-ticeably tender, golden pastry. Pudding heaven.

250g/10oz flour plus extra for dusting
250g/10oz butter plus an extra knob
3 tbsp natural yoghurt or water
100g/4oz sugar plus 1 tbsp
100g/4oz ground almonds
2 eggs
500g/1lb Victoria plums
splash of milk

Pre-heat the oven to 400F/200C/gas mark 6. Sift the flour into the bowl of a food processor or mixing bowl. Dice 150g butter directly into the flour and, if using a machine, pulse briefly, then add the yoghurt with the machine running. Once the pastry forms into a clump, it's done. Alternatively, rub the butter into the flour with your hands, mix in the yoghurt and form it into a ball. Rest the dough for at least 15 minutes, preferably 30, to avoid shrinking as it cooks.

Melt the remaining butter and stir with the ground almonds, 100g/4oz sugar and one beaten egg. Coarsely chop the plums and discard the stones. Divide the pastry into four equal pieces. Dust a work surface with flour and roll one pastry ball into a 15cm/6ins circle, using an upturned plate as a guide. Roll the other 5 pieces. Spoon the almond paste on one half of the circle of pastry, leaving a 2cm/1ins border. Pile plums on top and quickly paint the border with water, then fold the rest of the pastry over the filling. Press the edges together to seal and then, working from one end to the other, crimp with your fingers, rolling the pastry border upwards and forming little pleats, tucking neatly as you go. Tuck the ends underneath.

Mix the remaining egg with a splash of milk and paint the pasties generously, taking special care to 'glue' the edges. Dredge with sugar. Bake for 30 minutes.

Apricot and Goat's Cheese with Cardamom

Makes 4 pasties

This apricot pasty would be delicious without goat's cheese but it turns it into something very special indeed. It puffs and billows like a golden, flaky pillow and tastes both Moorish and moreish.

200g/8oz ready-to-eat dried apricots
1 tbsp runny honey
1 vanilla pod
8 cardamom pods or scant tsp ground cardamom
flour for dusting
300g/12oz ready-rolled puff pastry
150g/6oz soft goat's cheese such as Chavroux
2 tbsp peeled pistachios or blanched almonds
egg wash
1 tbsp caster sugar

Place the apricots in a pan with the honey, vanilla pod, cardamom and just enough water to cover. Bring to the boil, reduce the heat, half-cover the pan and simmer for 15 minutes until the apricots are soft and swollen and the juices thick and reduced. Scoop the apricots onto a plate to cool and drain about 4 tbsp of the thick, golden liquid into a mixing bowl. Mix in half the cheese.

Roll and cut 4 circles approx 15cm/6ins from the pastry. Leaving a 2.5cm/1ins border, spread the pastry circles with the remaining cheese. Pile the apricots on top of one half, and then spoon the apricot and cheese mixture over the top. Coarsely chop the nuts and scatter over the top. Moisten the border, fold over the pastry, press the edges together, then roll the edge towards the middle to seal and tidy. Crimp as before, then paint the entire surface with beaten egg. Make a few steam holes with a fork. Dredge with sugar and bake (400F/200C/gas mark 6) for 20 minutes until the pastry is puffed and golden. Serve hot, warm or cold with any remaining apricot juices in a little jug.

EQUIPMENT FOR PASTY MAKING

'Superstitious fishermen will never take a pasty on board a boat for fear that it will bring them bad luck'.
Cornish folklore

No special equipment is required for pasty making although one or two things will make the process easier. You'll need a rolling pin, obviously, but if you're caught short, a bottle will do. I use upturned saucers or plates as a template for cutting the circle of pastry.

I have two pastry brushes: one for painting the border with water and the other for glazing the pastry with egg. I use a wide metal palette knife or a very thin fish slice to lift the pasties onto the baking tray. I line the baking tray with non-stick baking parchment but have recently invested in a couple of non-stick 'cookamesh' baskets from *www.lakeland.co.uk (015394 88100)*. They sit directly on the oven shelf and ensure the pasty cooks evenly and the pastry browns without a soggy bottom. As a precaution, I usually lay a sheet of foil on the floor of the oven in case of leaks.

PASTY PASTRY

**Rough Puff
Empanada
Shortcrust
Food Processor Shortcrust
Suet**

'Promises and pie-crust are made to be broken.'
Jonathan Swift, Polite Conversation, 1738

Rough puff pastry, made by grating hard fat directly into strong white flour or plain flour, then mixing rather than rubbing the two together, before adding sufficient water to bind the dough, makes soft, stretchy pastry that is ideal for pasty making. Not only is the dough more malleable than usual, so it stretches over the plump filling, it also bakes up very crisp, almost like puff pastry. Pastry made with suet is also very good, although rich in taste and with a noticeably uneven texture. Most people, though, stick with regular short-crust pastry. Leaving it to sit for thirty minutes before rolling will help to make it stretchy.

Different fats affect the texture as well as the flavour of pastry. The crispest pastry is made with beef dripping, but lard or vegetable shortening, or a mixture of lard and butter and margarine, is good too. It's a matter of taste. Some people make pasties with wholemeal flour. I find the results hard and unappetising.

Always work with cold ingredients and touch the pastry as little as possible. When rolling the pastry, always roll away from yourself, turning the pastry as you go. Keep the rolling pin and work surface floured to prevent sticking. Make your pasties any size you like; large ones to feed a hearty appetite are usually made from an 20cm/8ins diameter circle of dough, medium ones 15cm/6ins, using a small plate or saucer as a guide.

Roll the pastry the thickness of a £1 coin unless the recipe specifies otherwise. Quantities given are sufficient for 4-6 pasties depending on size.

Rough Puff

250g/½ lb lard
400g/14oz strong plain flour
pinch of salt
4-6 tbsp ice cold water to mix

Place the piece of lard in its wrapper in the freezer and leave for about an hour until very hard.

Sift the flour and salt into a mixing bowl. Remove the lard from the freezer, peel back the paper, dip into the flour and grate it into the bowl, dipping back into the flour every now and again to make the grating easier. Now, mix the lard evenly into the flour by making sweeping scoops with a palette knife until it resembles heavy breadcrumbs. Stir in 1 tbsp water at a time until the dough clings together, then form into a ball. Place the dough in a polythene bag and chill in the fridge for 30 minutes before rolling.

Empanada

500g/1lb plain or maize (for Mexican flavour) flour
½ tsp salt
250g/10oz soft butter or lard
1 large egg yolk

Sift the flour and salt into a bowl and rub in the fat with your fingertips until the mixture is crumb-like. Add 1 egg yolk and about 3 tbsp water to bind to a stiff but kneadable dough. Roll into a ball, cover with clingfilm and chill for 1 hour.

Shortcrust

400g/14oz strong plain flour
pinch salt
100g/4oz cold lard or vegetable shortening
100g/4oz cold margarine or butter
4-6 tbsp ice cold water to mix

Sift the flour and salt into a mixing bowl. Cut the lard and margarine or butter directly into the flour in small chunks. Quickly rub it into the flour until the mixture resembles heavy breadcrumbs. Add the water, a little at a time, and use a rounded knife to stir it up into a clump. Knead a couple of times, pat the pastry into a ball, cover and set aside for 30 minutes.

Food Processor Shortcrust

Ingredients as for shortcrust recipe above

Sift the flour and salt into a food processor then cut the lard and margarine into small pieces on top of it. Process for 20-30 seconds, then add ice-cold water through the top, about 1 tbsp at a time, with the machine running. Once the pastry forms into a clump, it's done. Knead into a ball, wrap in clingfilm and chill for 30 minutes.

Suet

400g/14oz strong plain flour
200g/8oz Atora beef suet
pinch of salt
4-6 tbsp ice-cold water to mix

Sift the flour and salt into a mixing bowl. Stir in the suet and quickly rub it into the flour. Add the water, a little at a time, and use a rounded knife to stir it up into a clump. Knead a couple of times, pat the pastry into a ball, cover and set aside for 30 minutes.

_____

_____

_____

_____

_____

_____

_____

_____

_____

_____

_____

_____

_____

_____

_____

_____

_____

_____

_____

_____

PASTIES